The Less You Know, the Better You Sleep

Also by David Satter

*It Was a Long Time Ago and It Never Happened Anyway:*
*Russia and the Communist Past*

*Darkness at Dawn: The Rise of the Russian Criminal State*

*Age of Delirium: The Decline and Fall of the Soviet Union*

# THE LESS YOU KNOW, THE BETTER YOU SLEEP

## RUSSIA'S ROAD TO TERROR AND DICTATORSHIP UNDER YELTSIN AND PUTIN

### DAVID SATTER

Yale

UNIVERSITY PRESS

New Haven and London

Yale University Press books may be purchased in quantity for
educational, business, or promotional use. For information, please e-mail
sales.press@yale.edu (U.S. office) or sales@yaleup.co.uk (U.K. office).

Set in Adobe Garamond and Gotham types by IDS Infotech, Ltd.
Printed in the United States of America.

Library of Congress Control Number: 2015952182
ISBN 978-0-300-21142-9 (cloth : alk. paper)
ISBN 978-0-300-23072-7 (pbk.)

A catalogue record for this book is available from the British Library.

10 9 8 7 6 5 4 3 2 1

To the memory of the victims of the *Nord-Ost* theater siege, the Beslan school massacre, and the Russian apartment bombings

In the middle of the journey of our life, I found myself in a dark wood because the straightforward way had been lost. It is a hard thing to speak of. How wild, harsh and impenetrable that wood was, so that thinking of it re-creates the fear. It is scarcely less bitter than death: but in order to tell of the good that I found there, I must tell of the other things I saw there.

*Dante Alighieri,* Inferno

# Contents

## Preface to the Paperback Edition

In the hardcover edition of *The Less You Know, the Better You Sleep* I sought to give a truthful account of events in Russia that were either unknown or dangerously misunderstood. The book's reception, however, showed that in both Russia and the West the ignorance of pivotal events like the 1999 Russian apartment bombings was willful. Evil on such a scale is hard to grasp. It is easier to pretend it does not exist.

I was scheduled to give a talk about the book on January 19, 2017, at Sciences Po (the Paris Institute of Political Studies), one of the best universities in France. The lecture was announced but then abruptly canceled. I learned of the cancelation on January 9 from Thornike Gordadze, the research associate at the Center for International Research (CERI, a research center within Sciences Po) who had arranged the event. Sciences Po neither contacted me nor offered an apology. Another presentation was hastily arranged for January 23 at the offices of the journal *L'Esprit*, but it was too late to inform students at Sciences Po and members of the Russian, Ukrainian, and Chechen diasporas in France who wanted to attend. The cancelation did, however, attract the attention of the French press.

On January 27, *BuzzFeed* France reported that the lecture had been canceled out of fear of Russian retaliation. A source at Sciences Po told *BuzzFeed*, "The most likely scenario is that they feared for the academic exchange agreements with Russia. . . . I think that they also feared that their students studying in Russia might be expelled." This source said that after a conference on Chechnya in May 2016, Sciences Po received a complaint from the Russian embassy. "This time, they have censored themselves in advance."

Following the accusations publicized by *BuzzFeed,* roughly fifty CERI students gave the administration a letter of protest expressing surprise at the cancellation, citing the threat to academic freedom and demanding that I be reinvited.

On February 1 a new article appeared in *Le Monde.* Jean-François Bayart, the former director of CERI, protested the action of the current leadership. "The researchers at CERI see their independence regularly contested by authoritarian powers," he said. "It is hallucinatory to cancel a critical conference on Putin's Russia in the name of scholarly cooperation."

CERI's current director, Alain Dieckhoff, issued a statement denying that Sciences Po had self-censored or yielded to political pressure. He said the presentation of *The Less You Know* was canceled because Gordadze, an associate researcher, had not organized the event in collaboration with a permanent member of the institution. The school, he added, valued the development of a critical spirit; to suggest otherwise was "malevolent and false."

But on February 17, *Le Monde* published a note from Ewa Kulesza, the executive director of CERI, which revealed that Dieckhoff was not being truthful about the reason for the cancelation. "In the present context of tense relations," she wrote, "to invite a person to speak at CERI, who, no matter how good his publications, was expelled from Russia and in all probability is still under surveillance by . . . the [Russian] security organs looks extremely imprudent. We all know what things they are capable of, including in relation to

CERI." Kulesza said that although academic freedom is a high priority, there is sometimes a need to adopt a "reasonable approach."

The self-censorship at the institution charged with preparing France's political elite was not reciprocated with restraint on the Russian side. Having hacked into the computers of the Democratic Party in the United States in 2016, the Russians then mounted cyberattacks in France, as asserted by French experts. French President François Hollande called for a mobilization of "all means" to counter the threat of Russian interference in the French elections, scheduled for April 2017. On March 6, 2017, in an interview with major European newspapers, Hollande said Russia was trying to mislead Western public opinion by fostering the pretense that Russia was the defender of Christianity against attack by radical Islam. He called for an unmasking of Russian ideological operations. This included refuting Russian propaganda and identifying Russian financing of right-wing groups but not, if the example of Sciences Po is any guide, trying to tell the frightening truth about Russia itself.

The seemingly local event at Sciences Po in Paris provoked a strong reaction. *Le Canard Enchaîné, Le Figaro, The Times* (London), Radio Liberty, and Radio France International all wrote about the self-censorship of one of France's most prestigious institutions of higher learning. But the instinct to avoid the truth about Russia's recent history is hardly restricted to one school or to France. The United States has long practiced its own self-censorship over the role of terrorism in the creation of the present Russian regime. The Obama administration launched its "reset" policy despite convincing evidence that the Russian Federal Security Service (FSB) was behind the 1999 apartment bombings that brought Putin to power, and despite the fact that Putin was implicated in the murders of former

FSB agent Alexander Litvinenko and investigative journalist Anna Politkovskaya. Donald Trump, during his campaign, advocated a de facto alliance with Putin against terrorism, apparently unaware that he proposed fighting terror with someone who is a terrorist himself.

*The Less You Know* seeks to explain a crucial element of Russia's post-Soviet history, the role of terrorist attacks where there is evidence that the Russian government was involved. The most important attacks were the 1999 bombings. They were blamed on Chechen terrorists, but an unexploded bomb was discovered in Ryazan, southeast of Moscow, and the bombers were caught. They turned out to be agents of the FSB, not Chechens.

On February 8, 2000, U.S. Secretary of State Madeleine Albright, testifying before the Senate Foreign Relations Committee, was asked by Senator Jesse Helms (R-NC) whether there was any evidence linking the bombings to Chechnya. This was a critical question because the bombings were the justification for a Russian invasion of Chechnya and a new Chechen war. Albright said: "We have not seen evidence linking the bombings to Chechnya."

Helms then asked, "Do you believe the Russian government is justified when it accuses Chechen groups as responsible for the bombings?" Albright would say only, "The investigation into these bombings is ongoing." This answer came five months after the attacks and more than four months after the FSB agents were caught planting a bomb in Ryazan. "We condemned the deadly apartment bombings in the harshest terms," she continued. "Acts of terror, in all their forms, have no place in a democratic society."

Albright's avoidance of an answer on the question of responsibility for the bombings was all the more remarkable because the true situation was well reflected in the State Department's own reporting.

Shortly after the release of *The Less You Know* in spring 2016, I filed Freedom of Information Act (FOIA) requests with the State Department, the CIA, and the FBI requesting documents on the bombings and the incident in Ryazan, as well as on the murders of several persons who sought to investigate the Ryazan incident.

On November 30, 2016, I received several documents from the State Department in partial fulfillment of my request. One of them, a cable from the Moscow embassy, reports that a former Russian intelligence officer, apparently the embassy's principal informant, told an embassy political officer that the real story of the Ryazan incident could never be known because it "would destroy the country." He said the FSB had "a specially trained team of men whose mission is to carry out this type of urban warfare," meaning the bombing of buildings, and that Viktor Cherkesov, the first deputy director of the FSB and a former interrogator of Soviet dissidents, was "exactly the right person to order and carry out such actions."

In the face of such a charge from a trusted source, the United States should at least have asked publicly for an explanation of the inconsistencies in the Russian official account. By not doing so, the United States helped to bury responsibility for the bombings and to create the conditions for Vladimir Putin to become dictator for life. In subsequent years, when asked about the apartment bombings, ambitious American Russia specialists reacted with almost as much fear as vulnerable Russians, well aware that in administrations seeking to reset U.S.-Russia relations, too great an interest in the 1999 bombings might be lethal to their careers. Academics and journalists, with an eye to their visas and Russian contacts, have also found it easier to write about Russia without mentioning the apartment bombings.

Yet the world is still haunted by these bombings. On September 24, 2014, the youth wing of the opposition Yabloko Party held a conference in Moscow to mark the fifteenth anniversary of the Ryazan incident. After *The Less You Know* was published in 2016, the chapter on the apartment bombings was summarized in Russian by the banned opposition site Kasparov.ru.

Awareness has also increased in the United States. In 2015, PBS released a *Frontline* documentary called "Putin's Way" in which I was interviewed at length about the bombings. It was the first time, outside my own writing in *National Review* and the *Wall Street Journal,* that any mainstream media outlet accepted that the FSB had carried out the attacks. Two important books also appeared which supported the idea that Putin came to power through acts of terror. These were John Dunlop's *The Moscow Bombings of September 1999* and Karen Dawisha's *Putin's Kleptocracy.*

What was long missing in the United States was any serious effort at the political level to address the issue of Putin's terrorism against his own people. In a fundamental development, however, on January 11, 2017, Senator Marco Rubio (R-FL), raised the issue of the apartment bombings during the confirmation hearings for Secretary of State–designate Rex Tillerson. Only John McCain (R-AZ) had raised the issue previously, in 2003, in a more guarded fashion. Rubio's remarks were a sign that the bombings, ignored for so long, might finally become a subject of serious Western debate.

The West cannot afford to ignore such an atrocity, even many years after it occurred. The CIA, in response to my FOIA request, said that because of the need to protect "sources and methods," it could not provide documents or even acknowledge that the 1999 bombings were investigated. It needs to reconsider this decision. I believe the existing evidence establishes the FSB's guilt in blowing

Yet the world is still haunted by these bombings. On September 24, 2014, the youth wing of the opposition Yabloko Party held a conference in Moscow to mark the fifteenth anniversary of the Ryazan incident. After *The Less You Know* was published in 2016, the chapter on the apartment bombings was summarized in Russian by the banned opposition site Kasparov.ru.

Awareness has also increased in the United States. In 2015, PBS released a *Frontline* documentary called "Putin's Way" in which I was interviewed at length about the bombings. It was the first time, outside my own writing in *National Review* and the *Wall Street Journal*, that any mainstream media outlet accepted that the FSB had carried out the attacks. Two important books also appeared which supported the idea that Putin came to power through acts of terror. These were John Dunlop's *The Moscow Bombings of September 1999* and Karen Dawisha's *Putin's Kleptocracy*.

What was long missing in the United States was any serious effort at the political level to address the issue of Putin's terrorism against his own people. In a fundamental development, however, on January 11, 2017, Senator Marco Rubio (R-FL), raised the issue of the apartment bombings during the confirmation hearings for Secretary of State–designate Rex Tillerson. Only John McCain (R-AZ) had raised the issue previously, in 2003, in a more guarded fashion. Rubio's remarks were a sign that the bombings, ignored for so long, might finally become a subject of serious Western debate.

The West cannot afford to ignore such an atrocity, even many years after it occurred. The CIA, in response to my FOIA request, said that because of the need to protect "sources and methods," it could not provide documents or even acknowledge that the 1999 bombings were investigated. It needs to reconsider this decision. I believe the existing evidence establishes the FSB's guilt in blowing

CERI." Kulesza said that although academic freedom is a high priority, there is sometimes a need to adopt a "reasonable approach."

The self-censorship at the institution charged with preparing France's political elite was not reciprocated with restraint on the Russian side. Having hacked into the computers of the Democratic Party in the United States in 2016, the Russians then mounted cyberattacks in France, as asserted by French experts. French President François Hollande called for a mobilization of "all means" to counter the threat of Russian interference in the French elections, scheduled for April 2017. On March 6, 2017, in an interview with major European newspapers, Hollande said Russia was trying to mislead Western public opinion by fostering the pretense that Russia was the defender of Christianity against attack by radical Islam. He called for an unmasking of Russian ideological operations. This included refuting Russian propaganda and identifying Russian financing of right-wing groups but not, if the example of Sciences Po is any guide, trying to tell the frightening truth about Russia itself.

The seemingly local event at Sciences Po in Paris provoked a strong reaction. *Le Canard Enchaîné, Le Figaro, The Times* (London), Radio Liberty, and Radio France International all wrote about the self-censorship of one of France's most prestigious institutions of higher learning. But the instinct to avoid the truth about Russia's recent history is hardly restricted to one school or to France. The United States has long practiced its own self-censorship over the role of terrorism in the creation of the present Russian regime. The Obama administration launched its "reset" policy despite convincing evidence that the Russian Federal Security Service (FSB) was behind the 1999 apartment bombings that brought Putin to power, and despite the fact that Putin was implicated in the murders of former

FSB agent Alexander Litvinenko and investigative journalist Anna Politkovskaya. Donald Trump, during his campaign, advocated a de facto alliance with Putin against terrorism, apparently unaware that he proposed fighting terror with someone who is a terrorist himself.

*The Less You Know* seeks to explain a crucial element of Russia's post-Soviet history, the role of terrorist attacks where there is evidence that the Russian government was involved. The most important attacks were the 1999 bombings. They were blamed on Chechen terrorists, but an unexploded bomb was discovered in Ryazan, southeast of Moscow, and the bombers were caught. They turned out to be agents of the FSB, not Chechens.

On February 8, 2000, U.S. Secretary of State Madeleine Albright, testifying before the Senate Foreign Relations Committee, was asked by Senator Jesse Helms (R-NC) whether there was any evidence linking the bombings to Chechnya. This was a critical question because the bombings were the justification for a Russian invasion of Chechnya and a new Chechen war. Albright said: "We have not seen evidence linking the bombings to Chechnya."

Helms then asked, "Do you believe the Russian government is justified when it accuses Chechen groups as responsible for the bombings?" Albright would say only, "The investigation into these bombings is ongoing." This answer came five months after the attacks and more than four months after the FSB agents were caught planting a bomb in Ryazan. "We condemned the deadly apartment bombings in the harshest terms," she continued. "Acts of terror, in all their forms, have no place in a democratic society."

Albright's avoidance of an answer on the question of responsibility for the bombings was all the more remarkable because the true situation was well reflected in the State Department's own reporting.

Shortly after the release of *The Less You Know* in spring 2016, I filed Freedom of Information Act (FOIA) requests with the State Department, the CIA, and the FBI requesting documents on the bombings and the incident in Ryazan, as well as on the murders of several persons who sought to investigate the Ryazan incident.

On November 30, 2016, I received several documents from the State Department in partial fulfillment of my request. One of them, a cable from the Moscow embassy, reports that a former Russian intelligence officer, apparently the embassy's principal informant, told an embassy political officer that the real story of the Ryazan incident could never be known because it "would destroy the country." He said the FSB had "a specially trained team of men whose mission is to carry out this type of urban warfare," meaning the bombing of buildings, and that Viktor Cherkesov, the first deputy director of the FSB and a former interrogator of Soviet dissidents, was "exactly the right person to order and carry out such actions."

In the face of such a charge from a trusted source, the United States should at least have asked publicly for an explanation of the inconsistencies in the Russian official account. By not doing so, the United States helped to bury responsibility for the bombings and to create the conditions for Vladimir Putin to become dictator for life. In subsequent years, when asked about the apartment bombings, ambitious American Russia specialists reacted with almost as much fear as vulnerable Russians, well aware that in administrations seeking to reset U.S.-Russia relations, too great an interest in the 1999 bombings might be lethal to their careers. Academics and journalists, with an eye to their visas and Russian contacts, have also found it easier to write about Russia without mentioning the apartment bombings.

up the buildings beyond a reasonable doubt. But documents in the CIA files, which can be released with appropriate redactions, have the potential to make this guilt even more obvious.

Establishing the truth about how Putin came to power is important for both the United States and Russia. The apartment bombings show that for Russia's rulers domestic terror is an acceptable method of rule. In this respect, they differ little from those who place car bombs in crowded markets to polarize Shiites and Sunnis. It should go without saying that they cannot be partners in fighting terrorism.

At the same time, widespread knowledge of the truth about the bombings is necessary because it would blunt the Russian propaganda assault against the West. Even the most deluded Westerner would be sobered to know that the authors of that propaganda are capable of crimes far beyond anything of which they accuse the West. The talk of Putin as a defender of traditional values, popular in some conservative circles, would come to an end.

Perhaps most important, this knowledge would also lay the foundation for a genuine U.S.-Russia rapprochement. On the American side, it would mean no more self-deluding resets. Russians, meanwhile, would have the opportunity to understand their own history. The reality of Putin's path to power would demonstrate, more powerfully than any Western counterpropaganda ever could, the terrible cost of the Russian people's subservience to the state and the state's disregard for human life. It also can promote a set of values for both Russians and Americans that could help end the present dictatorship and lay the groundwork for Russia's moral and political resurrection.

# Preface

On December 23, 2013, I received word that the Russian Foreign Ministry had finally approved my visa and issued a number for my visa approval letter. I had been living in a rented apartment in Kiev while a revolution unfolded on the streets, writing a diary for Radio Liberty and other publications about the extraordinary events that were freeing a people and propelling the world to a new crisis.

Despite the fascination of events in Ukraine, I was anxious to bring the Russian bureaucratic process to an end. I had been waiting three weeks for the approval and wanted to return to Moscow where, after years of traveling back and forth from the United States, I hoped to settle for at least a few years. With the news of approval, all I had to do was go to the Russian consulate and present the number, along with a completed application and photograph.

On Christmas Eve, I went to the consulate and was buzzed in by staff members. The consul greeted me cordially and asked me to wait while he retrieved the approval letter. After an hour and a half, he returned and said that he had found my number in the consular log but that there was no letter. At my request, he searched for the letter twice more without success. Finally I asked him: "Has there ever been a case in your experience where the Foreign Ministry issued an approval number without an accompanying letter?" "No," he replied, "never."

Back in my apartment, I called the Foreign Ministry in Moscow and explained the situation to Lev Lvovich, a diplomat in the press department. He seemed surprised and said he would consult with his superior. A half hour later, he told me to call the embassy the following day and ask for Alexei Gruby, a first secretary. Something had gone wrong, he said, but Gruby would make sure I received my visa.

That night, my documentary film, *Age of Delirium,* about the fall of the Soviet Union, was shown in the Maidan Nezalezhnosti (Independence Square), the epicenter of Kiev's antiregime revolt. About a hundred people stood for an hour and forty minutes in subzero cold in an improvised outdoor cinema watching the story of the fate of ordinary people in the Soviet collapse. The next morning, I was interviewed by Kiev's Espreso TV, an internet television network that covers the Maidan. After the interview I called the embassy and was connected to Gruby.

Ukraine celebrates the Orthodox Christmas, so all offices, including the Russian embassy, were open on December 25. Gruby, who was expecting my call, said he had a statement to read to me: "The competent organs have determined that your presence on the territory of the Russian Federation is undesirable." My application to enter Russia had been refused. The phrase "competent organs" is used in Russia to refer to the Federal Security Service (FSB). The formula "your presence is undesirable" is used in espionage cases. I had never before heard it applied to a journalist.

The Russian authorities were not objecting to anything I had written. My previous stay in Moscow had been only three months, during which time I had been able to do little more than open a bank account, familiarize myself with the operations of the Radio Liberty Russian Service, where I was to serve as an adviser, and organize an apartment. The only significant article I had written concerned Yeltsin's destruction of the Russian parliament twenty years before, in 1993. Still, my expulsion was not a complete surprise. As Viktor Davidoff put it in the *Moscow Times,* it was not surprising that I was expelled; "it was amazing that it took so long."[1]

When I first began working in Russia, in 1976, as a correspondent for the London *Financial Times,* I quickly concluded that Russia was an alternate universe that could be understood only through the details of individual Russians' lives. These efforts led to an attempt to expel me in 1979 for "hooliganism." I survived that attempt because both the British and the American governments threatened to expel Soviet correspondents in retaliation, and I remained in the Soviet Union until 1982, when I left to write my first book, *Age of Delirium: The Decline and Fall of the Soviet Union.* It was this book that became the film shown on Christmas Eve in the Maidan.

During the 1980s, I was refused visas to the Soviet Union and was able to enter the country on reporting trips just twice, after the U.S. State Department threatened retaliation against Soviet correspondents if I was barred. In 1990, with perestroika under way, I continued to be blacklisted. I was apparently the last journalist still banned. But *Reader's Digest,* for which I was writing pieces about Russia, threatened to cancel plans for a Russian-language edition of the magazine. The Soviet authorities were encouraging Western institutions to set up in Moscow and, faced with the *Digest* ultimatum, decided to give in.

For the next two decades, I traveled freely to Russia, writing two books and hundreds of articles. In 1999, after four apartment buildings in Russia were blown up, killing hundreds of residents in their sleep and providing the pretext for starting the second Chechen war, which brought Vladimir Putin to power, I contended that the bombings were carried out by the FSB, not by Chechen rebels. I also argued that the decision in 2004 by Russian forces to open fire with flamethrowers on the gymnasium of the school in Beslan that had been seized by terrorists, killing 338 hostages, constituted a crime against humanity.[2]

Despite these stories, I regularly received visas, and persons connected to the Russian authorities pointed to me as an example of the regime's tolerance of free expression. In fact, this tolerance was based on the authorities' confidence in their ability to manipulate Western opinion. The picture of contemporary Russia sent back by Western journalists and academics was far from favorable, but it hardly conveyed how morally damaged Russia really was.

An example of the Russian success in manipulating Western observers was the Valdai Discussion Club, organized as a means of influencing the world's leading experts on Russia, both journalists and academics. One of the great attractions of the meetings was the opportunity to question Putin and other Russian officials in a supposedly informal setting. Russian officials were unfailingly generous with their time and hospitality, but they tightly controlled the proceedings, providing detailed answers to prepared questions and ignoring or giving short shrift to those that were even mildly critical. The participants, anxious not to offend their hosts for fear of not being invited back, engaged in self-censorship, as the Russian authorities knew they would. After the sessions, the participants in the "club" returned to the West, where they often cited their firsthand contact with Russian leaders and parroted what they were told.

The success of Valdai was reflected in headlines like the one on the BBC web site on September 20, 2013, the forum's tenth anniversary: "Putin shines at Valdai summit as he castigates the West."[3] The story described Putin's criticism of the West, in his opening speech, for losing touch with its Christian roots. Richard Sakwa, a British academic, was quoted as saying he would not participate in Valdai if it were simply "brainwashing." Instead, he said, the Valdai participants "felt the evolution, the self-confidence of this country, its consolidation," inadvertently demonstrating the effectiveness of that brainwashing.[4]

Russia's ability to manipulate foreign opinion, however, is limited by external circumstances. In December 2013, as I was waiting for my Russian visa to be renewed, the crisis in Ukraine was changing the calculus. The mask of liberalism had effectively misled the world about the true nature of the regime, but if the regime began to be directly threatened, as it was by events in Ukraine, it would have to take steps that would make the illusion harder, or impossible, to sustain.

I owed my continued presence in Moscow to the regime's desire to protect the masquerade. Russian officials liked to point out that no American journalist had been expelled since the end of the Cold War. With the Ukraine crisis, however, the authorities apparently decided that the show was over. My presence in Moscow was a luxury they could no longer afford.

Understanding Russia is actually very easy, but one must teach oneself to do something that is very hard—to believe the unbelievable. Westerners become confused because they approach Russia with a Western frame of reference, not realizing that Russia is a universe based on a completely different set of values. If a Westerner takes it for granted that the individual has inherent worth and is not just raw material for the deluded schemes of corrupt political leaders, he may not realize that in Russia this outlook is not widely shared. To grasp the reality of Russia, it is necessary to accept that Russian leaders really are capable of blowing up hundreds of their own people to preserve their hold on power. They really are capable of ordering an attack with flamethrowers on a gymnasium full of defenseless parents and children. Once one accepts that the impossible is really possible, the degradation of the Yeltsin years and Vladimir Putin's rise to power make perfect sense.

# Acknowledgments

In my effort to describe what went wrong in Russia after the fall of the Soviet Union, I was supported by a number of institutions without which this work would not have been possible. I would like to express my deep appreciation to the Sarah Scaife Foundation, the Smith Richardson Foundation, the William H. Donner Foundation, and the Earhart Foundation, and to Michael Gleba, Nadia Schadlow, Marin Strmeki, Ingrid Gregg, Montgomery Brown, and Curtin Winsor. I would also like to mention my longtime benefactor and friend Daniel McMichael, who died September 23, 2013.

My sons, Raphael and Mark, read early versions of the manuscript and provided helpful suggestions and comments. My thanks also to the Henry Jackson Society, which sponsored me for a British residency permit after I was expelled from Russia in December 2013.

# Abbreviations and Administrative Delineations

FSB     Federal Security Service

KGB     Committee for State Security

MVD     Ministry of Internal Affairs

Oblast     Often similar in size to an American state, an oblast is a territorial subdivision of the Russian Federation. Since 2004, the governors of oblasts have been appointed by the president.

SBU     Security Service of Ukraine

The Less You Know, the Better You Sleep

# 1

## The 1999 Apartment Bombings

In the summer of 1999, with the Boris Yeltsin era coming to an end, those at the pinnacle of power in Russia feared for their freedom and even their lives. There were signs of an economic recovery, but most citizens were still living in poverty and waiting months to be paid. The Yeltsin entourage was increasingly isolated and widely hated for its role in pillaging the country. According to Russians and Westerners with access to the Kremlin leadership, the leading members of the Yeltsin "family"—Tatyana Dyachenko, the president's daughter; Boris Berezovsky, her close adviser and the country's richest man; and Valentin Yumashev, a member of the Security Council and Dyachenko's future husband—lived in fear of a cruel reckoning. Many were convinced they would never surrender power.

In the twelve days from September 4 to the 16th, however, everything changed. Four apartment buildings were blown up in Moscow, Buinaksk, and Volgodonsk, and the controversies that wracked the country over corruption and privatization were suddenly forgotten. Eight years of post-Soviet Russian history was telescoped into the shocking images of bodies being carried out of the rubble of bombed buildings.

Newly appointed prime minister Vladimir Putin expressed perfectly the country's desire for revenge. On September 24, he said, "We will pursue the terrorists everywhere. If they are in an airport, then in an airport, and, forgive me, if we catch them in the toilet, then we'll rub them out (*mochit*) in the toilet. . . . The question is closed once and for all."[1]

Russian officials said there was a "Chechen trail" in the bombings.[2] The wording was unusual: not proof but a "trail." The Chechens insisted that they had nothing to do with the bombings,[3] and no proof of their involvement was ever adduced. But Russian forces were already fighting Chechen rebels in Dagestan, and the country was looking desperately for someone to blame. Russians had been opposed to further involvement in Chechnya, but in the wake of the apartment bombings, sentiment shifted.[4] They were now ready for a new Chechen war.

The mystery of who bombed the apartment houses in 1999 has never been solved. To the extent that there is evidence as to the perpetrators, it points not to Chechen terrorists but to the Kremlin leadership and the FSB.

When I was told on Christmas Day 2013 that the "competent organs" had determined that my presence in the territory of the Russian Federation was "undesirable," I was certain that my role in the investigation of the 1999 apartment bombings was the most important reason. Many journalists asked me, "Why did they decide to expel you rather than someone else?" The Russian authorities had tolerated my presence for ten years since the publication of my book *Darkness at Dawn: The Rise of the Russian Criminal State,* in which I accused the FSB of responsibility for the explosions. They did this, I believe, because my expulsion would have drawn attention to an episode the rest of the world seemed to have forgotten.

But by the time I worked in Moscow in late 2013, Putin's hold on power was weakening. Mass protests had taken place in Moscow and a popular revolution had broken out in Ukraine. The question of the apartment bombings had never quite gone away in Russia, and now the whispers were becoming louder. In the new conditions, raising the topic freely was not going to be allowed.

Yeltsin's Russia in the spring of 1999 was a nation traumatized by impoverishment and criminalization, and it was far from certain that the presidential elections set for June 2000 would take place. The popular approval ratings of both Yeltsin and his newly appointed prime minister and heir apparent, Vladimir Putin, were at 2 percent.[5] It was nearly inconceivable that anyone connected with Yeltsin could win a free election. But there was a widespread fear that Yeltsin would find a pretext for declaring a state of emergency so that the elections would not take place.

On June 6 of that year, Jan Blomgren, the Moscow correspondent for the Swedish newspaper *Svenska Dagbladet*, reported that a faction in the Kremlin was seriously weighing "terror bombings that could be blamed on the Chechens."[6] In the July 22 issue of *Moskovskaya Pravda*, the military journalist Alexander Zhilin quoted "trustworthy sources in the Kremlin" saying that persons close to Dyachenko were planning to use terror attacks in Moscow to discredit Yuri Luzhkov, the mayor of Moscow, who had emerged as one of Yeltsin's most serious political opponents. The plan was referred to as Storm in Moscow and was to include attacks on the headquarters of the FSB, the Interior Ministry (MVD), and the Federation Council, kidnappings by Chechen rebels, and a war between criminal gangs. All this was intended to create the impression that Luzhkov had lost control over the city.[7]

Also in June, Russia began a steady military buildup on the Chechen border. Significant numbers of artillery and aircraft were transferred to the region, followed in early July by the arrival of multiple-rocket launchers capable of destroying entire areas. The slow increase of forces continued until the equivalent of a Russian division, about seven thousand men, was on the border.[8]

At the same time, there were also puzzling developments in neighboring Dagestan. An invasion from Chechnya by Islamic rebels was widely expected. But in late spring, the Russian authorities surprised local law enforcement by withdrawing internal troops stationed on the border, clearing a route for would-be invaders.

On August 7, the invasion took place. An Islamic force of twelve hundred armed men, commanded by the Chechen leader Shamil Basaev and an Arab extremist named Khattab, entered Dagestan from Chechnya without meeting any resistance. A high-ranking MVD official later said that if the internal troops had not been withdrawn, the invasion would not have been possible.[9] The invaders occupied territory in the Botlikh region and were fought mostly by local self-defense units. On August 23, the invaders withdrew, again without encountering resistance. A Russian commander told a correspondent for *Time* magazine that during the retreat, he had Basaev in his sights but was ordered to hold his fire. "We just watched Basaev's long column of trucks and jeeps withdraw from Dagestan back to Chechnya under cover provided by our own helicopters," he said. "We could have wiped him out then and there, but the bosses in Moscow wanted him alive."[10]

The Chechen government condemned the invasion. Aslan Maskhadov, the Chechen president, tried to reach Yeltsin on a hotline installed after the first Chechen war, but no one answered. Within a few days, the line went dead.[11]

After the rebels had withdrawn, Russia bombed the Botlikh region for several days and then began a punitive operation against

Karamakhi-Chabanmakhi, an enclave that a year earlier, with official permission, had proclaimed Islamic law. Russian forces surrounded villages and bombed them, killing up to one thousand civilians.[12] There was no obvious connection between the Botlikh events and Karamakhi-Chabanmakhi, which is in a different part of Dagestan.

In response to the bombing of Karamakhi-Chabanmakhi, on September 4, Basaev's forces reinvaded Dagestan, leading to fighting that continued for almost three weeks. The apartment bombings occurred while this fighting was going on. The timing of the bombings coincided with the fighting in Dagestan, creating the impression that the bombings were revenge for the attacks by the Russian military on Islamic insurgents in Dagestan.

The invasion of Dagestan was treated by the Russian government as a sign that the Chechens wanted to take over the entire North Caucasus. In August, however, the investigative weekly *Versiya* published a report indicating that Basaev's invasion of Dagestan had been organized with Russian complicity. According to the weekly, Alexander Voloshin, the head of the presidential administration, had met with Basaev on July 4 in the town of Beaulieu, between Nice and Monaco, at a villa belonging to the international arms merchant Adnan Khashoggi. This information was said to come from a source in French intelligence. On September 13 and 14 the newspaper *Moskovsky Komsomolets* published parts of the transcript of a friendly conversation between a man with a voice similar to that of Boris Berezovsky—Yeltsin's daughter's close adviser—and Movladi Udugov, the unofficial spokesman for the radical Chechen opposition, which included Basaev and Khattab. In the conversation, they appeared to discuss the transfer of money to the radicals.[13]

These publications may have inspired Vitaly Tretyakov, the editor of Berezovsky's most important publication, *Nezavisimaya Gazeta,* to offer a version of events that slightly defended Berezovsky while agreeing that the incursion into Dagestan was organized by the authorities. "It is perfectly obvious," Tretyakov wrote, "that the Chechens were lured into Dagestan . . . in order to provide a legitimate excuse for . . . beginning the offensive phase of struggle against the terrorists grouped in Chechnya. Clearly it was an operation by the Russian special services . . . that was, moreover, politically authorized from the very top." As for Berezovsky, whose voice was apparently captured on tape offering to pay the radicals, Tretyakov speculated that he may have been used "without his knowledge by the Russian special services." It was more than likely, Tretyakov wrote, "that he acted in coordination with them," a possibility he considered "far more realistic than the theory that Berezovsky 'set everything up.' "[14]

During this fateful summer when Moscow was awash with rumors, I was friendly with a Russian political operative who was well connected to the higher levels of Russian power. When I met him, he told me about the growing fear in the Kremlin about the possibility of the Yeltsin government's losing power and the rumors that Moscow would be the scene of a huge provocation. He said that the issue was the security of Yeltsin and his family in the case of a handover of power. If there was no agreement on terms, "they will blow up half of Moscow."

I sensed the uneasiness but did not know how to assess my friend's prediction. I had no illusions about Yeltsin and his cronies, but it was hard to imagine that a man who came to power through a peaceful anticommunist revolution with massive public support would murder his own people to hold on to power. Developing events were to change my mind.

At 9:40 PM on September 4, a truck bomb exploded in Buinaksk, Dagestan's second-largest city. It destroyed a five-story apartment building that housed soldiers from the 136th Motor Rifle Brigade. The explosion occurred while many residents were at home, watching a televised soccer match between France and Ukraine, and dozens of persons were buried under the rubble. The eventual death toll was sixty-four, with nearly one hundred people injured.

It later transpired that the toll could have been much worse. Hours after the first explosion in Buinaksk, a second bomb was discovered in a ZIL-130 truck near the military hospital. Sappers stopped a watch mechanism twelve minutes before the bomb was set to explode. There was almost six thousand pounds of explosives in the truck, enough to have leveled the central part of the city.

The events in Buinaksk, although major, did not stun the nation because the victims were Dagestani, not Russian, and Dagestan was a war zone. On September 9, however, the terrorists struck again, this time in Moscow. Shortly after midnight, a bomb exploded in the basement of a building at 19 Guryanova Street, in a working-class area in the southeast part of the city. The central section of the building was obliterated, leaving the left and right stairwells standing on each side of a gaping hole. Fires raged for hours under the rubble. "It's like hell underneath," one rescuer said. "Even if they survived the blast, they would have been burned alive."[15] In the end, 100 people were killed and 690 injured.[16] Russian officials blamed the bombing on Chechen terrorists seeking revenge for their "defeat" in Dagestan. The Moscow FSB announced that items removed from the scene showed traces of TNT and hexogen, a powerful military explosive.

Four days later, on September 13, an explosion at 6 Kashirskoye Highway in Moscow flattened a nine-story brick apartment building, turning it into a pile of rubble. To add to the horror, the explosion took place at 5 AM, when almost all of the residents were asleep. Muscovites awoke to graphic television footage showing emergency workers feverishly going through the debris. The death toll was eventually established at 124, with 7 injured.[17]

The Russian capital was now gripped by unspeakable terror. Every one of the city's thirty thousand residential buildings was ordered to be checked for explosives;[18] residents organized round-the-clock patrols. There were thousands of calls to the police reporting suspicious activity.

On the morning of the explosion on Kashirskoye Highway, Gennady Seleznev, the speaker of the State Duma, announced at a meeting of the Duma Council that on the previous night, an apartment house had been blown up in the city of Volgodonsk. The significance of this announcement would not become clear until later.

On September 16, the terror spread. With funerals of the Moscow victims still going on, a truck bomb exploded in Volgodonsk. The blast ripped off the façade of a nine-story apartment building. The dead bodies of eighteen people, including two children, were pulled from the rubble. Eighty-nine were hospitalized. This explosion, like the one on Kashirskoye Highway, took place at 5 AM. The psychological shock was so great that afterward hundreds of people were unwilling to sleep in their homes and insisted on spending the night outdoors. The bomb left a crater 11.5 feet deep and forty to fifty feet wide. Parts of the vehicle that carried the bomb were dispersed over a radius of nearly a mile.[19]

The Volgodonsk bombing appeared to mean that there would now be attempts to bomb apartment buildings in cities outside of

Moscow. This expectation was borne out, but with surprising consequences.

At 8:30 PM on September 22, Alexei Kartofelnikov returned home to his apartment in Ryazan, a city 120 miles southeast of Moscow, after a weekend at his dacha. He noticed a white Lada parked in front of the building at 14/16 Novoselov Street with a male passenger in the back seat. The last two numbers on the car's license plates were covered with pieces of paper that had "62," the code for Ryazan, written on them. Kartofelnikov went up to his apartment and called the police. His daughter, Yulia, a twenty-three-year-old medical intern, went out onto the balcony and watched as a man emerged from the basement, checked his watch, and got into the car, where two people were waiting. In the meantime, another resident, Vladimir Vasiliev, returned and also noticed the car. The piece of paper with "62" on the rear license plate had now fallen off so that the number on the car's rear plate was different from the number on the front. He also called the police.

When the police arrived, Yulia insisted that they check the basement. The basement had been used as a toilet by local derelicts, so they did not want to go down there. But they finally agreed, went down the steps, and immediately ran back up shouting, "There's a bomb." The building was soon engulfed in chaos. Police began going door to door telling residents to leave. People took babies out of bathtubs, grabbed documents, and threw on overcoats. Those too ill or weak to leave the building were left behind.

As residents watched on the street, the police, including Yuri Tkachenko, the head of the local bomb squad, entered the basement. Tkachenko disconnected a detonator and timing device and then tested three sacks of a white crystalline substance with a portable gas analyzer. The contents of the sacks tested positive for hexogen, the same substance used in the previous apartment bombings. There now was no question that someone had tried to blow up the building.

The sacks were taken out of the basement at around 1:30 AM and driven away by the FSB. But the FSB agents forgot to take away the highly professional military detonator, which was left in the hands of the bomb squad. It was photographed and time-stamped the next day.

On the basis of descriptions by Kartofelnikov, his daughter, and Vasiliev, the police prepared identikit portraits of the suspects. The railroad stations and airport were cordoned off, and roads leading out of the city were blocked.

The white Lada was found around dawn, abandoned in a parking lot. A short time later, a call to Moscow was made from a public telephone in Ryazan, and the operator who connected the call caught a fragment of the conversation. The caller said there was no way to get out of town undetected. The voice on the other end replied, "Split up and each of you make your own way out."[20] The operator reported the call to the police, who traced the number. To their surprise, it belonged not to Chechen terrorists but to the FSB. The terrorists were soon arrested, and to the stupefaction of the police, produced FSB identification. The FSB ordered them released.

The FSB now had no choice but to offer some explanation. On Friday, September 24, FSB director Nikolai Patrushev came out of a Kremlin meeting and announced that the evacuation of the building had been part of a training exercise.

Patrushev's statement contradicted what the authorities had been saying for two days. On the morning of the 23rd, Alexander Sergeev, the head of the Ryazan FSB, had appeared on television and congratulated residents on being saved from a terrorist attack. Vladimir Rushailo, the interior minister, announced on national television that an attempted terrorist act had been foiled. But now Patrushev said the incident was a test. The sacks found by the bomb squad contained sugar, and the reading that indicated hexogen was a mistake.

There were similar exercises in other cities, Patrushev said, but only in Ryazan did the people react promptly. He complimented the residents on their vigilance.

These events provoked anger in Ryazan, where people had spent the night of September 23 sleeping outdoors. Journalists raised the possibility that those responsible for the four previous bombings were also not Chechens but the FSB. Society, however, did not react in an organized fashion. The day after the bomb was discovered, Russian aircraft began bombing the Grozny airport, in Chechnya, and on October 1, Russian troops moved across the border, launching the second Chechen war.

It was anger over Hitler's "treacherous attack" on the Soviet Union that helped mobilize the Soviet people in the first days of World War II, and since then that attack has been a touchstone in the Russian popular consciousness. The bombings played a similar role. For the vast majority of Russians, the Chechens had carried the war to the Russian people and now had to pay a price. The Ryazan episode, though disturbing, was forgotten in the rush of fast-moving events.

Five years earlier, the first Chechen war had begun with the slaughter of Russian troops trapped in their tanks in the narrow streets on Grozny on New Year's night, 1994–95. This time, the invasion of Chechnya was carried out methodically and seemingly with success. In its wake, Putin's popularity soared. Only 2 percent of the population had favored him for the presidency in August, and in

September just 4 percent. In October, the number reached 21 percent. In November, Putin was favored for the presidency by 45 percent of Russians, far more than preferred any other candidate.[21] It was now clear that there would be no need to introduce emergency rule and postpone the elections. Putin could win on his own, with the help of a new war.

Russian forces easily advanced over the Chechen lowlands to the Terek River. They then stopped and conducted strikes into other parts of Chechnya. In December, they crossed the Terek, surrounded Grozny, and began a massive bombardment that left the city looking like Stalingrad.

In early October, I met again with the operative who had warned me of a massive provocation coming in Moscow; he said the apartment bombings were that provocation. This was not an isolated view. Many Russians newspapers were making the same charge, especially the mass circulation *Moskovsky Komsomolets,* the newspaper *Novaya Vremya,* and the weekly newspaper *Obshchaya Gazeta.* It was characteristic of Moscow's mood under Yeltsin that after eight years in which the country had been run for the benefit of gangsters and oligarchs, the idea that the authorities had organized a terrorist act against their own people seemed not only plausible but likely.

"The perpetrators," my friend said, "planted the [Guryanov Street] bomb in a workers' area, not in an elite area in the center of town. If the perpetrators were Chechens and the purpose was to make a political point, blowing up ordinary people was senseless.

"If you look at a map of Moscow, you see that for a terrorist, the choice of place was idiotic. A terrorist should be able to get out quickly. Pechatniki [where the Guryanov Street building was located] is a peninsula. On three sides is the Moscow River and the only way out is Ryazansky Prospekt.

"This is also the poorest region of Moscow. It has the cheapest apartments and the worst ecology. The second blast was on the Kashirskoye Highway, also among the cheapest, flimsiest houses in Moscow.

"The explosive that was used was hexogen. This is the reactive agent for a new generation of artillery shells in Russia. There is only one factory that produces hexogen. It is in the Perm oblast and it is tightly guarded by the FSB. Every gram is registered.

"In order to produce this kind of destruction, hexogen has to be weighed and the bomb strategically placed. This can be done only by specialists. The explosives were put in precise locations, and the buildings collapsed like a house of cards."

I was impressed. The bombings had created terror in Russia and then, having provided a justification for a new war in Chechnya, they abruptly stopped. At the same time, the sites were cleared of debris, including body parts, within three or four days, effectively destroying the crime scenes.

I was almost certain that my friend's information was coming from disaffected members of the security services. I asked him to arrange for me to talk to his informants, and he promised to arrange a meeting. The following day I received a call and agreed to meet two men in front of the Bolshoi Theater at 6 PM.

The men were in their thirties. We went to a nearby department store, got into an elevator, and got off at an upper floor. We then walked down to a landing with a view of the square. It was already dark, the columns of the Bolshoi were illuminated, and streetlamps were burning in the square. There was a light rain.

The men said they were meeting me out of respect for my friend. They said there was indeed something strange about the apartment bombings.

As the two spoke, I took no notes, relying on my memory. We gave the impression of three men having a talk. Nonetheless, I glanced around continuously for the appearance of an interested on-looker. The two men elaborated on the information given by my friend. They said that the idea that the bombings were carried out by Chechen terrorists did not make sense. All four bombings had the same "handwriting," attested by the nature of the destruction, the way the buildings' concrete panels collapsed, and the volume of the blasts. The explosive in each case was said to be hexogen, and all four bombs were timed to go off at night to assure the maximum number of casualties.

To have carried out such a campaign, Chechen terrorists would have needed a major logistical operation. They would have had to prepare nine explosions (four that took place and five that the Russian authorities claimed to have prevented) in widely distant cities in the space of two weeks. This would have had to be done, moreover, while the Chechen Islamists, the preferred suspects, were engaging Russian forces in Dagestan and the official Chechen government was bracing for a Russian invasion. Under these circumstances, the Chechens could not have gained access to tons of hexogen from a factory in the Perm oblast that was tightly guarded by the central FSB.

The two men elaborated on my friend's statement that the bombers had to have been highly trained specialists. In Moscow, they told me, the first bomb caused the entire central section of the building to collapse. On Kashirskoye Highway, an eight-story brick building was reduced to rubble. To produce this kind of result, it was necessary to identify and destroy the critical structural elements. This requires training. The only sources of such training in Russia were the Special Forces, military intelligence (GRU), and the FSB.

The bombings were explained as a response to the Russian attacks in Dagestan after the Chechen-led Islamist invasion of Dagestan in August. But a careful model of events showed that it would have taken four to four and a half months to organize the bombings. The bombers had to select and visit the targets, make corrections, determine the optimum mix of explosives, order their preparation, make final calculations based on the makeup of the explosives, rent space in the targeted buildings, and transport the explosives to the targets. Planning would have had to begin in the spring, well before the Chechen invasion of Dagestan. The attacks might, however, have been part of a bigger plan that included the Chechen invasion of Dagestan, the Russian bombing of the Islamist villages in "retaliation," and the bombings in Buinaksk, Moscow, and Volgodonsk, which could then be depicted as the revenge of the Chechens. Such a plan could have been implemented only by elements of the Russian government in cooperation with the FSB.

This information struck me as very convincing. In addition to the obstacles Chechen terrorists would have faced in carrying out the bombings, it was hard to see how the explosions could serve their purposes. Their only real result would have been to justify a new invasion of Chechnya. But the bombings clearly served the interests of the Yeltsin entourage, which was hoping to control the presidential succession and, in that way, stay out of prison.

On September 30, General Alexander Lebed, who had run for president in 1996, said in an interview with the French newspaper *Le Figaro* that he was virtually certain the Yeltsin family was behind the apartment bombings. "Any Chechen commander who wanted revenge would have begun to blow up [Russian] generals. He would have struck at the buildings of the Ministry of Internal Affairs or the FSB or at weapons storage areas or at atomic electric power stations. He would not have chosen to target simple and innocent people. A goal had been set—to create mass terror." Lebed was asked whether the Kremlin clan was ready for anything. "For anything to hold on to power," he said. "All means are good."[22]

By October, I had heard enough to put my suspicions into an article, which I entitled "Anatomy of a Massacre." I had lost contact with U.S. editorial pages after the fall of the Soviet Union, and those relations had only been partially restored. I was also uncertain who would be willing to publish an article suggesting that the leading candidate for the Russian presidency was a terrorist. But I had recently established contact with the *Washington Times,* which, under Clinton, was widely read in Washington for its oppositionist coverage. I decided to send the article there.

I was also leaving for the city of Krasnoyarsk, the scene in the 1990s of the bloody battles for control of the aluminum industry in which dozens of people were murdered. I knew that I would later travel by car from Krasnoyarsk to Sayansk, a journey of five hours on a road that went through miles of snow-covered taiga, where cars were easily stopped and people sometimes disappeared without a trace.

Thinking over what to do, I studied the October 22, 1999, issue of *Moskovsky Komsomolets,* which had entire pages filled with pictures of the bombings' victims. At the top of one page was a photo of the building on Guryanov Street with lights burning in all the windows. I began studying the faces of the victims. Who were they? I looked at the picture of the Mikhailin family, Sergei and Tatyana and their two children, Zhanna, twenty-four, and Alexander, sixteen. They lived in apartment 97. In the photo, Zhanna is leaning with her head on the head of her brother. The parents are looking on calmly and, I thought, proudly. The entire family was killed.

The next page showed victims of the explosion of the building on Kashirskoye Highway. Felix Misharin, fifty-eight, of apartment 74, had been snapped in a celebratory mood. He stood with his right arm extended and his left arm around his wife, Vera, fifty. On the same page was a photo of the debris in which the Misharins were buried when the bomb that had been hidden in the basement went off. What to do? Ignore all this? I wrote an email to the editorial page of the *Washington Times,* attached my article, and pressed send. I then left for the airport and the night flight to Krasnoyarsk. The article appeared the next day in the *Washington Times*—and was ignored.[23]

Such an article would not have been unusual in the Russian press at the time, but despite a flurry of initial reports about the strange events in Ryazan, attention in the West to the apartment bombings soon all but disappeared. For the next fifteen years, the policies of the Western powers were based on the assumption that questions about the Putin regime's legitimacy did not exist.

On September 14, the day after the first Moscow bombing, Putin said that the security services were certain of the participation of Osama Bin Laden in the bombings. Nikolai Patrushev, the director of the FSB, said that the organizers of the bombings were "international terrorists dug in in Chechnya with the connivance of the official powers in Grozny."[24] These statements helped many in the West to accept the idea that the apartment bombings were carried out by Islamists.

Critical to the credence given in the West to official Russian explanations was an inability to accept the idea that the Yeltsin regime would murder hundreds of its own citizens and terrify the nation to hold on to power. This refusal to believe the unbelievable, however, came at a cost. It crippled Western policy toward Russia, rendering it naïve and ineffectual. From the moment Putin took power, the West maintained an image of Russia that bore no relation to reality.

Russia held parliamentary elections in December 1999. The groundswell of support for Putin and the new war in Chechnya transformed the political landscape. The Unity Party, which was created on the advice of Berezovsky and had no platform besides support for Putin, achieved a striking political success. Yeltsin, as president, had confronted an oppositional parliament, but the pro-Putin forces achieved a strong parliamentary majority, leaving the opposition without a political base in the national government. On New Year's Eve, Yeltsin resigned and Putin was named acting president, giving him the advantages of incumbency. In accordance with the Constitution, elections were moved up from June to April, and the presidential campaign was launched.

While this was going on, Russian journalists began to reexamine the incident in Ryazan. Pavel Voloshin, a thirty-year-old reporter for *Novaya Gazeta,* went to the Ryazan Ministry of Internal Affairs (GUVD) in early February and met with Yuri Tkachenko, the sapper who had tested the bomb. Tkachenko would later be barred from contact with journalists, but on this occasion he gave a detailed interview in which he insisted that the bomb found in the basement at 14/16 Novoselov Street was real. He said it had a genuine military detonator, and the state-of-the-art gas analyzer used by the Ryazan police clearly indicated the presence of hexogen.

Voloshin also talked to the police officers who answered the original call from Kartofelnikov. They too insisted that the incident was not an exercise, and that the substance in the bags did not look anything like sugar.

Drawing on these and other interviews, Voloshin published an article in the February 14 issue of *Novaya Gazeta* under the headline "Sugar or Hexogen? What Happened in Ryazan." In addition to reporting the views of Tkachenko and others, Voloshin suggested that the FSB publish the order for the exercise and give journalists access to the agents who had placed the bomb in the basement and to the material evidence.[25]

The article provoked wide discussion but little reaction from officials. One afternoon shortly after it was published, however, Voloshin received a call at the office of *Novaya Gazeta* from a teacher who said that one of her female students had a girlfriend who met a soldier who bragged about guarding sacks of hexogen. The soldier, Alexei Pinyaev, was based in Naro-Fominsk, outside of Moscow. Voloshin drove to the base, entered secretly, and succeeded in meeting with the soldier.

Pinyaev said that in the autumn of 1999, he was sent from a base in the Moscow oblast to the base of the 137th Ryazan paratroop regiment, twenty miles from Ryazan, where paratroopers were prepared for fighting in Chechnya. After a period of shooting and parachute jumping, he was assigned to guard a warehouse that supposedly contained arms and ammunition. Guard duty was tedious, and Pinyaev and another soldier decided to look inside. They opened the metal door, but instead of weapons, they saw a pile of 110-pound sackcloth bags labeled "sugar."

Pinyaev said that they were puzzled as to why it was necessary to stand guard over bags of sugar, but not wanting to leave empty-handed, they stuck a bayonet into one of the bags and poured out some of the sugar into a plastic packet. Later they made tea with it. Pinyaev said the taste was revolting and they feared they had poisoned themselves. They took the plastic bag to their commander. He called a bomb expert, who tested it and told the commander that the substance in the bag was hexogen.

Almost immediately, Pinyaev and the other soldier were relieved of their normal duties and began to be called regularly for interrogations. To their astonishment, they were berated not for stealing sugar but for "divulging state secrets." Their fellow soldiers advised them to prepare for long prison sentences. In the end, however, the matter was closed and the FSB officers advised Pinyaev and the other soldier to forget about the warehouse and the "special sugar."

Pinyaev's story was published in the March 13 issue of *Novaya Gazeta* under the headline "Hexogen. FSB. Ryazan." For the first time, it was alleged that on the eve of the supposed training exercise, a large quantity of hexogen was being kept under guard on a military base twenty miles from Ryazan, in sackcloth bags labeled "sugar."[26]

On March 17, in the wake of the *Novaya Gazeta* publication, Yuri Shchekochikhin and Sergei Ivanenko, two deputies from the liberal Yabloko parliamentary faction, urged their colleagues in the State Duma to demand from the general procurator answers to the following questions:

1. At what stage was the criminal case opened in connection with the discovery in Ryazan of an explosive substance, September 22, 1999?
2. Was any analysis of the substance carried out?
3. Who gave the order to carry out such "exercises" and to have them use either real or imitation explosive substances?

The deputies also suggested that the Duma demand that the general prosecutor check the facts published in *Novaya Gazeta* about the storing of hexogen in the guise of sugar in an arms warehouse at a training camp for paratroopers.

The proposal failed because the 197 yes votes fell 29 votes short of an absolute majority. The Unity party voted unanimously against. The proposal was rejected a second time on March 31, this time by a vote of 104 for and 133 against.[27]

The misgivings raised by the *Novaya Gazeta* articles, however, grew so widespread that they led the FSB to agree to participate in a televised meeting between its top officials and residents of the building in Ryazan. The purpose of the program, which aired on NTV on March 23, 2000, was to demonstrate the FSB's openness, but FSB officials instead gave the opposite impression: that they were trying to conceal something terrible.

Nikolai Nikolaev, the host of the program, asked Alexander Zdanovich, the spokesman for the FSB, how it was possible that Sergeev had mistaken a dummy for a real bomb.

"General Sergeev," Zdanovich explained, "is not a sophisticated expert in the matter of explosive devices."

Sergeev, however, was only communicating what had been told him by Tkachenko. Zdanovich was therefore suggesting that the bomb squad was incompetent.

Nikolaev asked Raphael Gilmanov, an independent explosives expert in the hall, whether it was possible to mistake sugar for hexogen.

"No one who saw hexogen in his life would ever confuse it with sugar," Gilmanov said.

"Do you allow for the possibility of a false reading by the gas analyzer?" Nikolaev asked.

"No."

Nikolaev then asked about the legality of the supposed exercise.

Pavel Astakhov, a lawyer representing a group of residents of the building, said that the law on investigative activities covering military exercises did not give the FSB the right to mine a residential building and endanger the lives and health of Russian citizens. Moreover, article 5 of the law explicitly mentions the necessity of observing civil rights while carrying out exercises. A military man in the audience called the circumstances extremely suspicious. He said that the organization of military exercises is always accompanied by the preparation of ambulances, medicine, bandages, and warm clothing, and even the important exercises are always agreed upon with the local authorities.

Nikolaev asked why the investigation into the incident was continuing six months later.

"The FSB is assigned to investigate cases of terrorism," said Astakhov. "But the case can be closed by a prosecutor. If it was sugar in those bags, the case should have been closed a long time ago."

Zdanovich tried to answer the charges. "We are ready for discussion," he said. "This is why we are here. The exercise was intended to guard the security of citizens. We did this because we had no choice. We never acted against the people." As the meeting ended, however, and Ryazan residents and FSB officials filed out of the hall, it was clear that the FSB had suffered a major setback. That the FSB officials realized this was clear from their grim expressions.[28]

The broadcast of the meeting on March 23, a week before the presidential election, had a powerful effect. People everywhere were struck by the ineptitude of the FSB representatives' attempts to defend the organization's actions, and the program left the overwhelming impression that the incident in Ryazan resembled not a military exercise but a failed provocation.

In the short run, however, none of it seemed to matter. Three days after the broadcast, Putin was elected president of Russia.

With Putin's election, the authorities seemed to feel that they need no longer be concerned about the apartment bombings. The voices in the press that had raised the issue gradually fell silent, and it began to appear that the bombings would become just the last in the long list of unsolved crimes that defined the history of twentieth-century Russia. The issue was not irrelevant for me, however. Although I feared it was an exercise in futility, in April, a week after Putin's election, I decided to go to Ryazan.

In April 2000, Ryazan was a haunted city. The residents of 14/16 Novoselov Street suffered from heart problems and depression as a result of what happened, and their children were afraid to go to sleep at night. Those walking in and out of the building on the rainy night when I arrived there were completely convinced that the previous September's events were not a training exercise. One woman said that the authorities were fighting for power, and the lives of the people in the building were "not worth one kopeck."

"What should I believe," said Ivan Kirilin, a sixty-seven-year-old resident of the building, "what the government says, or what was in the basement?"

Some residents said that they were considering filing suit against the FSB. Others were more cautious. "The general opinion is that we'd better not challenge them," said Tatyana Lukichyeva, "or next time, they will really blow us up."

The residents of 14/16 Novosyelov Street resemble the working-class residents of any Russian city. The building was built in 1987 by the Ryazan radio factory and still houses many of its employees. For the most part, the residents are patriotic citizens. But the "exercise" and the events that followed it left them plagued by questions that would not go away. They wanted to know why, if the incident was a test, they were not allowed to return to their apartments after the bomb was successfully neutralized, and why they were not told of the real nature of the incident for two days. They also wanted to know what right the FSB had to make them guinea pigs in an exercise—if, indeed, it was an exercise.

I spoke to Vasiliev in his apartment. He was still trying to come to terms with what had happened.

"When I think that this building could have been blown up and not only I and my family but many of the people I've known for years could have been buried under piles of rubble, the idea just doesn't register."

I remarked that the victims of the bombings in Buinaksk, Moscow, and Volgodonsk also probably could not have imagined that they would be killed in their sleep.

"Who can imagine such a thing?" he asked. "It doesn't conform to any human logic. But the claim that it was a test makes no sense. Does it make sense to test people for vigilance at a time when the whole country is in a state of panic?"

Vasiliev said that the residents considered suing the FSB but gave up in the face of the daunting paperwork. "To file a case," he said, "each resident of the building would have had to write out his complaint individually. You need a lawyer for this and someone has to pay for it. When people realized how much was involved, they gave up. After what happened, no one had the time or strength."

The building on Novoselov Street was an odd choice for a test of vigilance because there was an all-night grocery store in the building and residents could have assumed that someone unloading sacks of sugar was doing so for the store. At the same time, the impact of the test would have been minimal because the building was at the edge of the city. But it was very well suited to be the target for a terrorist attack, especially if the goal was the maximum number of victims. Like the building on Kashirskoye Highway in Moscow, 14/16 Novosyelov Street was a brick building of standard construction. In an explosion there would have been little chance for anyone to survive. Because the building was also on an elevation, an explosion would have caused it to hit the adjacent building with the force of an avalanche, probably toppling it too. In this way, the tragedy in Ryazan would have eclipsed all the others.

In February 2002, a motion to investigate the Ryazan events failed in the State Duma for the third time. This time the vote was 161 in favor and only 7 opposed, but an absolute majority—226 votes—was required: the rest of the deputies were either absent or abstained.

With the realization that no official body was going to demand the truth about the bombings, a group of Duma deputies and human rights activists organized an independent commission to seek answers. The chairman was Sergei Kovalyev, a Duma deputy and former Soviet dissident who had once been Yeltsin's human rights chief. Sergei Yushenkov, another Duma deputy, was the vice chairman. The commission had no official standing, but it included prominent people, and the Duma deputies could direct questions to the government in their individual capacity.

But the commission members were fighting a rising tide of indifference. Putin gave the impression of prosecuting the second Chechen war successfully, and an economic boom that started before he took office was gaining momentum. His popularity rose to an all-time high.

Shortly after the independent commission began its work, however, an incident occurred that reminded Russians of just how mysterious the apartment bombings were. In March, the newspaper *Noviye Izvestiya* announced the result of its investigation into the fact that Gennady Seleznev, the speaker of the Duma and a close associate of Putin, had announced the bombing in Volgodonsk on September 13, three days before it occurred.[29]

Vladimir Zhirinovsky, the head of the Liberal Democratic Party, had informed journalists of what Seleznev had said about an explosion in Volgodonsk immediately after he said it. But they could not confirm his remark, so it was not reported. On September 16, however, the building in Volgodonsk really was blown up, and on the 17th, Zhirinovsky demanded an explanation.[30]

"Do you see what is happening in this country?" he said, shouting and gesticulating. "You say an apartment building has blown up on Monday and it explodes on Thursday. This can be evaluated as a provocation." Seleznev avoided responding, and when Zhirinovsky persisted, his microphone was turned off.[31]

Now the newspaper succeeded in getting the transcript of what Seleznev had said on the 13th. His precise words were: "Here is a communication which they transmit. According to a report from Rostov-on-Don today, this past night, an apartment house was blown up in the city of Volgodonsk." The newspaper asked Seleznev who had told him about the Volgodonsk bombing three days before it happened. He answered, "Believe me, not Berezovsky," thus indicating that he was well aware who had given him the information.[32]

Seleznev then told the newspaper that he had actually been referring to an explosion on September 15 that was organized by criminal gangs and did not claim any victims. This explosion was confirmed by the local Volgodonsk press, but Seleznev's explanation raised more questions than it answered.[33] It was hard to understand why, at a time when apartment buildings were being blown up with hundreds of casualties, it was necessary to inform the speaker of the Duma about such an insignificant incident. It was also odd that Seleznev did not mention the "routine" explosion in September 1999, when questions about his knowledge of the Volgodonsk bombing were first raised. And even if the note that he read concerned a genuine criminal conflict in Volgodonsk, he was still reporting on September 13 about an event on the 15th. How could he know about it two days in advance?

Alexander Litvinenko, a former FSB officer who had fled to London and was raising questions about the apartment bombings, offered a more plausible explanation. The note to Seleznev, in Litvinenko's opinion, was the result of "the usual 'Kontora' [FSB] messup. The explosion on Kashirskoye Highway was scheduled for the 13th and the Volgodonsk bombing for the 16th but they got it the other way around." Litvinenko said he later learned that the person who brought Seleznev the note about the Volgodonsk explosion was from the FSB, "just as I thought."[34]

As efforts were being made in Russia to investigate the apartment bombings, a new source of accusations against Putin and the FSB emerged in London. Boris Berezovsky, who had been instrumental in facilitating Putin's rise to power but then went into exile after being deprived of influence, held a press conference on March 5, 2002, in which he accused the FSB of carrying out the bombings with Putin's complicity in order to justify the second Chechen war. He presented the testimony of Nikita Chekulin, a former acting director of the Russian Explosives Conversion Center, a scientific research institute under the Ministry of Education, who was recruited by the FSB as a secret agent. Chekulin stated, and confirmed with documents, that in

1999–2000 a large quantity of hexogen was purchased by the institute from various military units and then, under the guise of gunpowder or dynamite, shipped all over the country to unknown destinations. Berezovsky also showed a documentary film, *Assassination of Russia,* made by two French producers who had originally worked with NTV to expand the program in which Nikolai Nikolaev questioned FSB spokesman Alexander Zdanovich.

Berezovsky's role was ironic. The apartment bombings took place while Putin was prime minister and Nikolai Patrushev, his longtime protégé, was the head of the FSB. But the planning for such a complex operation would have had to have begun much earlier, before Putin became prime minister, at a time when Berezovsky was one of the most powerful members of the leadership. Berezovsky played a critical role in advocating Putin's ascent and was also instrumental in promoting the new Chechen war, which made it possible for Putin to win the presidency. But the new Chechen war could not have happened without the apartment bombings. It is therefore hard to imagine that Berezovsky was not involved in them.

Berezovsky's attitude toward Putin changed only when Putin acted to remove him from power. Berezovsky started to hint and then in December 2001, two years after the explosions, to state openly that the apartment bombings were carried out by the FSB with Putin's complicity. This level of cynicism, though shocking by Western standards, is perfectly plausible for Russian leaders. Putin was not in a position to respond to the accusations by saying that Berezovsky was the real initiator and that he (Putin) was merely a passive participant. He would later accuse Berezovsky of responsibility for every major political murder and terrorist act that took place in Russia, but on the apartment bombings he had to remain silent. In the words of the Russian publicist Andrei Piontkovsky, "The more hopeless became [Berezovsky's] chances of returning to the political arena in Russia, the louder became his accusations. . . . It seems that he opened a completely new form of political business: Blackmail the authorities with the exposure of one's own crimes."[35]

Berezovsky's new role did not help uncover those responsible for the apartment bombings. Instead, his odious reputation made it easier for the authorities to avoid discussing the issue. The charge that the apartment bombings were a provocation became the "Berezovsky argument." Although the French film was only 25 percent financed by Berezovsky, it was described in Russia as the "Berezovsky film." FSB officials, when they commented on the bombings at all, said that they did not intend to enter into polemics with Berezovsky.

The independent commission began its work in February 2002 but could not get answers to its questions. Russian officials simply refused to respond even though, in the case of inquiries from deputies, responding was a legal obligation. Nonetheless, the commission achieved one important success. This came about after it had all but ceased to function, as a result of the activities of its investigator, a former FSB agent and orthodox communist, Mikhail Trepashkin.

Despite most commission members' distrust of Berezovsky, Yushenkov and Yuli Rybakov, a Duma deputy from St. Petersburg, flew to London to attend the March 5 press conference and watch the film. In London, Yushenkov met Litvinenko, who introduced him to Trepashkin. Trepashkin had been fired by the FSB after investigating the links between FSB officers and Chechen organized crime figures. After this meeting, Trepashkin began cooperating with the public commission.

In April, Yushenkov traveled to the United States and met Alena and Tanya Morozov, whose mother was killed in the explosion on

Guryanov Street. The Morozov sisters were officially crime victims. This meant that they could gain access to the investigation and participate in court proceedings. Tanya Morozov agreed to give Trepashkin her power of attorney.

The person who rented the basement storage area where the bomb was placed had presented the passport of Mukhid Laipanov, a resident of a village in the Karachaevo-Cherkesiya republic in the North Caucasus. It turned out, however, that the real Laipanov had been killed in an auto accident in February 1999. The police asserted that the person using his passport was Achemez Gochiyaev, an ethnic Karachai and the director of a Moscow construction firm whose warehouses were used as a transfer point for shipments of hexogen disguised as bags of sugar.

In fact, Gochiyaev was an unlikely suspect. He owned a home in Moscow, lived not far from where the bombing took place, and had many relatives in the city. If he had committed an act of terror against innocent civilians, he would have been putting his relatives at risk.

In the immediate aftermath of the Guryanova Street bombing, Mark Blumenfeld, the building superintendent, gave a description of the person who had rented the basement. The FSB released a composite photo of the suspect based on that description. It was briefly allowed to circulate, but then quickly replaced with one of Gochiyaev, who looked completely different. When Gochiyaev saw that he was being accused of blowing up a building, he immediately went into hiding.[36]

At the end of March 2002, Yuri Felshtinsky, the coauthor with Litvinenko of a book, *Blowing Up Russia,* that dealt with the apartment bombings, received a call from an unknown caller who said he was acting on behalf of Gochiyaev. At the end of April, the two authors handed a courier a list of questions for the person claiming to be Gochiyaev. Several days later, in another European country, an intermediary turned over a videotape and several photographs establishing Gochiyaev's identity, along with his handwritten testimony. In the statement, Gochiyaev insisted that he had been set up and had fled only because he knew that the FSB was getting ready to kill him.

Trepashkin found Gochiyaev's testimony convincing and decided to concentrate on locating the original composite photo. By this time, he was working closely with the independent public commission.

On the night of April 17, 2003, I was working in my Moscow apartment when I received a call that Sergei Yushenkov had been shot dead in front of the entrance to his apartment building. My book *Darkness at Dawn,* in which I argued that the FSB was responsible for the apartment bombings, was due out in the United States in May. Now Sergei, who held the same view and was trying to prove it, had been murdered. He was one of the most active members of the public commission on the bombings and had been full of enthusiasm when I saw him in a hallway of the State Duma only a few months earlier. He had told me of plans to circulate the French documentary and make people aware of the real story behind the bombings. I went to the window and looked at the surrounding buildings, the streetlamps, and the nearly empty street. For the first time in twenty-seven years of writing about Russia, I felt afraid to leave my apartment.

Yuri Shchekochikhin, another member of the public commission, died three months later, the victim of a mysterious illness that caused his skin to peel off and his internal organs to collapse. The Russian authorities refused to allow an autopsy, but his relatives managed to send tissue samples to London, where Shchekochikhin was tentatively diagnosed as having died from thallium poisoning. Thallium is also believed to have been used in the poisoning of Roman Tsepov, Putin's former bodyguard, in September 2004.

Shchekochikhin had been my friend since the 1980s. Shortly before his death, he presented me with a copy of his latest book, *Slaves of the KGB: 20th Century, the Religion of Betrayal,* about people forced to work in Soviet times as informers for the KGB. He had inscribed it: "We are still alive in 2003!"

With the deaths of Yushenkov and Shchekochikhin, Trepashkin was the only person still actively investigating the apartment bombings. As the lawyer for Tanya Morozova, he was entitled to review the FSB file on the case; he used this privilege to search for the first sketch of the prime suspect. He could find no trace of the picture, leading him to think it had been removed from the file and references to it had been expunged. So he began going through old newspaper archives in the hope that a picture had been published somewhere before the FSB pulled it from circulation. After an exhaustive search, he finally found a copy of the photo. To his surprise, it depicted someone he knew: Vladimir Romanovich, an FSB agent who in the mid-1990s had been responsible for ties with Chechen criminal organizations.

In those years Trepashkin had worked for the department of the FSB that protected officers, their sources, and their families. This gave him indirect knowledge of the operations of Chechen extremists who were being sheltered by Russian law enforcement. In 1995, he learned that a Chechen criminal band was engaged in shaking down banks in Moscow, including the Soldi Bank. Romanovich, who specialized in banks and had helped the Chechens rent a number of premises in Moscow for extortion and money laundering, had been a member of this group.

Trepashkin set up an ambush at the Soldi Bank, but the Chechens did not appear. Someone had tipped them off. He later learned that on the day of the failed ambush, a special vehicle ordered by

Romanovich was monitoring the bank. Trepashkin wanted to interrogate Romanovich, but the investigation was halted by Nikolai Patrushev, the head of his unit, who blocked further work on the case. It was explained to Trepashkin that the persons arrested were "our own Chechens." Patrushev later became the head of the FSB and held that post at the time of the apartment bombings.

Trepashkin began looking for the source of the portrait. He found Mark Blumenfeld, the former property manager. Blumenfeld said that on the morning of the bombing, he described the man who had rented the basement space to local police. This was the basis of the first composite photo. Two days later, he was brought to the Lefortovo, where FSB officers pressured him to change his story and "recognize" another photo, that of Gochiyaev.[37]

Trepashkin now was in a position to discredit the official explanation of the bombings. In September 2000, Viktor Zakharov, the head of the FSB for Moscow and the Moscow oblast, said: "We know the entire chain. At the head stands the not unknown [Arab] Khattab. Under his leadership were two demolition instructors, the Arabs Abu Umar and Abu Zharaf. They trained the saboteurs and provided them with explosives. The direct organizer of the terrorist acts was Achimez Gochiyaev, known in Chechnya under the nickname, 'The Fox.' He also led the perpetrators of the terrorist acts. All of them are adherents of the radical current of Wahhabism." He added that according to their information, Gochiyaev had received $500,000 from Khattab.[38]

But if the original sketch of the person who reserved the basement storage area was not of Gochiyaev, it was hard to see on what basis he was a suspect.

At this time, a trial was being prepared in the case of Yusuf Krymshamkhalov and Adam Dekkushev, two members of what the authorities were calling the "band of Gochiyaev" who had allegedly transported explosives to Volgodonsk. Trepashkin was preparing to present this new and dramatic evidence in court, but, aware of the risk he was taking, he first shared Blumenfeld's name and telephone number with Igor Korolkov, an investigative reporter for *Moskovskiye Novosti*. Korolkov met with Blumenfeld in the newspaper's office, and he confirmed that the man "who was making use of the Laipanov passport, and who was publicly presented by the investigation as Gochiyaev, was not in fact Gochiyaev."[39]

In a taped statement in the editorial office, Blumenfeld described what happened. "In Lefortovo Prison," he said, "they showed me a photograph of a certain person, and they said that it was Gochiyaev and that I had supposedly rented the basement to him. I answered that I had never seen this man. But it was insistently recommended to me that I identify Gochiyaev. I understood everything and ceased arguing and I signed the testimony. In point of fact, the person whose photograph was shown to me and who they called Gochiyaev was not the person who had come to me."

Korolkov asked Blumenfeld whether Gochiyaev and the person who came to him resembled each other. Blumenfeld said, "On the photo there was depicted a man with a simple face but the person who had come to me and to whom I had rented the premises looked externally like an intellectual. I formed the impression that he was a Jew. Moreover, a Jew with Caucasus roots. And I declared that more than once to the investigation."[40]

One day after his meeting with Korolkov, Trepashkin was arrested and his apartment was searched. He was charged with possession of an unlicensed gun, but a judge immediately dismissed that charge. He was then accused of improper use of classified material and was sentenced to four years in a labor camp in the Ural Mountains. His evidence was never presented in court.

After his arrest, Trepashkin was able to transmit to *Moskovskiye Novosti* notes that described the secret document he had supposedly improperly handled. He explained that he gave his former colleague, Colonel Shebalin, the transcript of an eavesdropped conversation among members of the Golyanovsky criminal organization in which it was said that past and present FSB agents were members of the group and took part in killings. Trepashkin said that the documents he was charged with publicizing could not bear the stamp "secret" because the law on state secrets prohibits classifying information about illegal acts committed by officials.

With Trepashkin's arrest, the investigation of the apartment bombings entered a lull. Those who wanted to raise the issue lacked investigative tools such as subpoena power and knew that too active an interest could cost them their lives.

Against this background, I unexpectedly emerged in Russia as one of the Putin regime's principal accusers. *Darkness at Dawn* was published in May 2003, and a month later, I presented the book in Washington at the Hudson Institute. The day before that event, I received an email from Alexander Goldfarb, an émigré whom I knew from Soviet dissident circles in Moscow in the 1970s, who was now working as an aide to Berezovsky. He asked whether I had any objection to the presence of a "German film crew" at my talk. I said I did not, and Goldfarb arrived with a husband-and-wife filmmaking team, Andrei Nekrasov and Olga Konskaya, and Alena Morozova, whose mother had died in the bombing on Guryanova Street and whose sister had given Trepashkin power of attorney to investigate the case.

In my presentation, I explained why I believed the apartment bombings were a provocation intended to assure Putin's accession to power. My remarks became part of a film, entitled *Disbelief,* which premiered in 2004 at the Sundance Film Festival. A Russian-language version was put on YouTube and circulated on DVDs in Russia. *Darkness at Dawn* was also translated into Russian, with long excerpts published in the press.

Unfortunately, the people capable of helping to make the bombings a serious political issue were disappearing. In 2004, Anna Politkovskaya, Russia's leading investigative journalist, called on the Russian presidential candidates to answer the outstanding questions surrounding the apartment bombings. Alexander Litvinenko continued to update his book and speak out on the case in London. Politkovskaya was shot dead in the elevator of her apartment block on October 7, 2006. Litvinenko died of radiation poisoning on November 23 after ingesting radioactive polonium, which was put into his tea in a London sushi restaurant.

The deaths of so many persons who had investigated the apartment bombings, all of them with the exception of Litvinenko my personal friends, left me as one of the few people still arguing that this monumental provocation could not be ignored. On May 17, 2007, testifying before the House Foreign Relations Committee on Russia's foreign policy, I explained the role played by the apartment bombings. In a widely quoted passage, I said this:

> With Yeltsin and his family facing possible criminal prosecution, a plan was put into motion to put in place a successor who would guarantee that Yeltsin and his family would be safe from prosecution and the criminal division of property in the country would not be subject to reexamination.
>
> For "Operation Successor" to succeed, however, it was necessary to have a massive provocation. In my view, this

provocation was the bombing in September 1999 of the apartment buildings in Moscow, Buinaksk and Volgodonsk. In the aftermath of these attacks, which claimed three hundred lives, a new war was launched against Chechnya. Putin, the newly appointed prime minister who was put in charge of that war, achieved overnight popularity. Yeltsin resigned early. Putin was elected president and his first act was to guarantee Yeltsin immunity from prosecution. In the meantime, all talk of re-examining the results of privatization was forgotten.[41]

For this I received some odd recognition. When Russia's First Channel screened a "documentary" alleging the September 11 attacks in the United States were orchestrated by the U.S. government, the station invited me to appear on air to comment on the film. I declined.

When I moved back to Russia in September 2013 to work as an adviser and contributor to Radio Liberty, I had no immediate plans to raise the issue of the apartment bombings. But I thought the subject would come up eventually.

In fact, the apartment bombings are impossible for a conscientious observer to ignore. The circumstantial evidence that the bombings were carried out by the FSB is overwhelming. The only reason there is no direct evidence is that the Putin regime has concealed it. The rubble from the bombings was cleared almost immediately, despite the objections of the Ministry of Internal Affairs (MVD) and the Ministry of Emergency Situations. The haste with which the crime scenes were destroyed is all the more striking when one considers that after U.S. embassies were bombed in Kenya and Tanzania in

1998, suspects were identified and eventually arrested as a result of the careful sifting of the rubble from the explosion, a process that went on for months.

In the case of the Ryazan incident, the authorities have sequestered the people who put the bomb in the basement, records of the exercise, and the "dummy" bomb itself. This has been done on grounds of secrecy. Yet article 7 of the Russian Federation law on state secrets, adopted July 21, 1993, states that among the things that cannot be classified as state secrets or declared to be secret evidence is information about "extraordinary accidents and catastrophes threatening the security and health of the citizens and their consequences . . . facts about the violation of the rights and freedoms of citizens . . . [and] facts about the violations of the law by state organs and officials."[42]

The greatest barrier to accepting the evidence that points to the FSB as the perpetrator of the bombings is not that it is unconvincing but that it is so difficult to believe such a thing possible. By any standard, murdering hundreds of randomly chosen civilians in order to hold on to power shows a cynicism that cannot be comprehended in a normal human context. But it is fully consistent with the kind of country that Russia, in the wake of communism, has become.

Russia has never really forgotten the apartment bombings. During the anti-Putin protests in 2011 and 2012, demonstrators carried signs referring to the attacks. The evidence that the bombings were a provocation means that Russia is carrying a burden that will weigh on it for years to come. Until the truth about the apartment bombings is known, the true nature of Russia's postcommunist history cannot be established. At the same time, failing to react to the evidence that the bombings were a government-planned mass crime leaves such provocation as a standing temptation for government leaders. If those responsible are not identified and punished, it will be assumed by those fighting for power in Russia that provocations are a legitimate way to win elections.

It is common in Russia for people to avoid certain issues because otherwise "it will be impossible to live." Unfortunately, the issues don't disappear. Of all the dangers that hang over Russia, none is more menacing than the failure to demand answers to the mystery of how Putin came to power.

# 2

## Yeltsin: Chaos and Criminality

Many things changed after the fall of the Soviet Union. But as society was rapidly transformed, it became obvious that there had been no moral revolution in Russia. Communist society had taken it for granted that the individual was expendable; postcommunist Russia did as well, often to an even greater degree. Yeltsin was a hero to many Russians after he successfully led the resistance to the August 1991 pro-communist coup. But neither Yeltsin nor the "young reformers" whom he put in charge of Russia's transformation showed any understanding of the need to establish the rule of law and the habits of respect for the individual. For Yeltsin and the reformers, the goal was to reach a "point of no return," beyond which it would be impossible to restore socialism regardless of the will of the people. Property had to be put into private hands as quickly as possible, and this was done with little regard for who received the property or on what basis. Capitalism was created. But by carrying out the largest peaceful transfer of property in history without the benefit of law, the reformers created the conditions for the criminalization of the whole country.

The new society that emerged had three outstanding characteristics: an economy dominated by a criminal oligarchy, an authoritarian political system, and, perhaps most important, a moral degradation that subverted all legal and ethical standards and made real civil society impossible. Their interaction set the stage for Russia's drift into a regime of aggression and terror.

If one were to choose a date for the beginning of the reforms, it would be January 2, 1992. On that day, just nine days after Mikhail Gorbachev's resignation marked the end of the Soviet Union, the government of the newly emerged Russian Federation, led by deputy prime minister Yegor Gaidar, abruptly freed prices. Gaidar predicted that prices would increase by a factor of three to five and then begin to fall. Instead in ten months, they rose by a factor of twenty-five to thirty.[1] By April, almost all the money in people's savings accounts— money saved for decades—had disappeared.

One night in Moscow in March 1993, there was a knock at the door of my apartment. I opened the door to a haggard old woman I had occasionally seen in the elevator. "Vera Pavlovna on the seventh floor has died," she said. "We're collecting money to pay for her funeral." Surprised by the request and stunned by the implications, I reached for my wallet for money to help bury this unfortunate, unknown woman. Scenes like this were being played out all over the country.

The wiping out of citizens' savings was followed by the appearance of numerous pyramid schemes that promised to help Russians survive the spiraling inflation. With no experience of the capitalist world, Russians were subjected to deceptive advertising campaigns that explained how their investments would grow. At first, as share prices rose steadily, the firms allowed investors to cash out their earnings, the better to attract new gamblers. Long lines formed as people fought to take advantage of the new opportunities. Soon, however— sometimes in as little as three months—the pyramid schemes stopped honoring their commitments. With the first decline in the volume of share purchases, the organizers took the investors' money and disappeared.

While hyperinflation drove millions into poverty, the well connected found numerous ways in the chaos to amass vast unearned wealth. One way to do so was to obtain low-cost government credits. Inflation created a shortage of turnover capital, which paralyzed production. To rescue the economy, credits were issued to industry at rates of 10 to 25 percent even though the inflation rate was 2,500 percent. The intent was to help factories pay salaries and purchase supplies, but instead of being used for this purpose, the credits were deposited in banks at commercial rates of interest. Bank officials and factory directors then split the profits.[2]

A second path to wealth was to obtain permission to export raw materials. Although most prices had been freed, energy prices, which at first were less than 1 percent of world market prices, continued to be regulated. The government, having abandoned the Soviet-era monopoly on foreign trade, allowed anyone to export who could get a license. Since raw materials were bought at the internal price, for rubles, and sold abroad at the world price, for dollars, export licenses were a license to print money. The Ministry of Foreign Economic Ties granted them in return for bribes. The fee for the license was insignificant next to the size of the bribe.[3]

A third source of wealth was subsidized imports. In the winter of 1991, fearing a famine, the government sold permits for the importation of food products at 1 percent of their real value, with the difference subsidized with the help of Western commodity credits. The products were sold at normal market prices, with the result that the attempt to relieve the country's food crisis led to the enrichment of a small group of traders. The value of import subsidies in 1992 came to 15 percent of the gross domestic product.[4]

After hyperinflation, the second factor that facilitated the rise of Russia's criminal oligarchy was the process of privatization. The placing of state assets in private hands actually began during perestroika, as officials took over government agencies and reorganized them as private businesses. In place of ministries, they organized "concerns." In place of the state distribution system, they created commodity exchanges, and in place of state banks, they created commercial banks. The buildings, suppliers, and personnel remained the same, but the organization's assets became the property of the new "owners."

Officially, privatization started in October 1992 with the widespread distribution of vouchers. Beginning that month, any Russian citizen could receive a state privatization check denominated at ten thousand rubles. Each voucher supposedly represented a citizen's share of the national wealth. Factories were converted into joint stock companies, and citizens were invited to exchange their vouchers for shares in any enterprise.

Most Russians had no idea what to do with their vouchers. Some used them to buy shares in their own factories. Others invested them in supposed voucher funds that advertised widely and promised dividends. Many vouchers were sold on the street, often for as little as ten dollars or a bottle of vodka. Mysterious persons who looked like vagrants appeared at bus stops and metro stations with cardboard signs saying "I buy vouchers." Their deliberately shabby appearance was meant to create the impression that the vouchers had no real value. Watching this spectacle in 1993 and 1994, I also formed the impression that the vouchers were worthless. But corrupt business and organized crime groups were behind the vagrants, and through them the first private property was created legally in Russia—and the first fortunes.

When auctions were held for shares in industrial enterprises, members of these groups arrived with packs of vouchers. In one of the first major investment auctions in 1993, a 4.88 percent ownership stake in the Sayansk Aluminum Factory was obtained by the firm Aluminproduct. It was run by Oleg Deripaska, who would become one of Russia's richest men. As a student at Moscow State University, Deripaska reportedly stood outside the entrance to the Khakassia factory, offering to buy vouchers from workers. Two years later he was the head of the factory.[5] Another oligarch, Kacha Bendukidze, through his company Bioprocess, was able to enter the auction for the giant Uralmash machine-building factory in Yekaterinburg. He presented 130,000 vouchers ten minutes before bidding was closed, obtaining 18 percent of the shares.[6] By some estimates, a few people who grasped how the voucher privatization game was played secured a third of the country's industrial base for $1.2 billion.[7] As for the rest of the population, in most cases their investments produced nothing.

Some people never invested their vouchers. Grigory Yavlinsky, the leader of the opposition Yabloko Party, would say later: "My voucher is at home. I'm saving it in order to show it one day to my grandsons as an example of how it is possible in a manner that is economically ineffective and politically illiterate to carry out privatization."[8]

In the latter part of 1994, voucher privatization was succeeded by privatization for cash. By now there was a group that could participate in it. Voucher privatization produced at least five oligarchs, Mikhail Fridman, the head of the Alfa Group; Deripaska; Vladimir Bogdanov, the head of Surgutneftegas; Bendukidze; and Vladimir

Potanin, through his firm Microdin, which worked actively in the privatization market.[9] Several others became billionaires by appropriating state resources with the help of corrupt connections: Mikhail Khodorkovsky (currency operations), Boris Berezovsky (automobiles), Valdimir Gusinsky (real estate), and Alexander Smolensky (banking).

Many of the newly rich set up banks, and these banks began to be "empowered" to handle government accounts. The official rate of return on the government's money was not high, but what mattered was that empowered banks, ignoring instructions that were not enforced anyway, treated budgetary funds as free capital that was available for investment. They delayed payment for months, often using the money for short-term interbank credits that were given at rates as high as 400 percent. Meanwhile, nonpayment of salaries became the reality of millions of Russians' lives.

It was this new group of millionaires and billionaires who, in the second stage of privatization, were able to buy up Russia's mines and factories for a fraction of their value. During cash privatization, enterprises were officially sold at auction, but the auctions frequently took place only on paper. In cases where they were actually held, officials of the State Property Committee often eliminated bidders or provided information about competing offers to the predetermined winner. Only rarely was there true competitive bidding, and if a powerful group was outbid by an insistent competitor, the winner could easily pay for his tenacity with his life.

The prices at which enterprises were sold stunned Russian society: 324 factories were sold at an average price of less than $4 million each. Uralmash was sold for $3.73 million, the Chelyabinsk Metallurgical Combine went for $3.73 million,[10] and the Murmansk Trawler Fleet, which had hundreds of ships, was sold for just $2.5 million.[11]

On September 9, 1994, the bulletin "Independent Strategy" reported: "The greater part of the basic productive funds of Russia are being sold for somewhere around $5 billion. Even if one considers that in Russia, the price of the basic means of production is equal to her gross domestic product [in the West, it usually is at least 2.6 times higher] . . . in effect, 300 to 400 billion dollars, the sum realized in privatization is minimal. For this reason, the agency recommends English investors not to miss the chance and to take part in the purchase of Russian enterprises."[12]

In late 1994, in response to pressure from the World Bank to reduce inflation, the Russian government ceased printing money. In order to meet its obligations, it launched the "loans for shares" program, which made possible the creation in Russia of companies comparable in size to the largest American corporations.

Under the program, the government mortgaged shares in the most desirable nonprivatized enterprises in return for loans. In theory, the program provided for competition. In practice, the shares went to powerful banks with the best "informal" connections to the government. The banks organized auctions in which they participated and which they inevitably won. Once an enterprise had been mortgaged, the proprietary bank was free to exploit it, and when the government failed to repay the bank loans (which, given the state's revenue shortage, was always the case), the enterprise became the lending bank's property.

The loans for shares auctions resembled a play. Once the auction began, a previously unknown firm would offer a bid that was almost identical to the starting price, which had been set by the bank that was named to organize the bidding. This established that the bidding was "competitive." The organizing bank could then, after ruling out other bids on various pretexts, offer a bid that was slightly higher than that of its "competitor." It thereby effectively set the price at which it would buy the enterprise.

Norilsk Nickel, the giant metals combine, was offered at a starting price of $170 million. Oneximbank, which was running the auction, won it with a bid of $170.1 million.[13] Oneximbank thus acquired a 38 percent share of the plant that produced 90 percent of Russia's nickel, 90 percent of its cobalt, and 100 percent of its platinum. In the course of three weeks, the government put into private hands enterprises that generated a fifth of the federal budget, including, besides Norilsk Nickel, some of the country's leading oil companies: Lukoil, Sindako, Surgut-Neftegaz, Yukos, and others.[14]

Loans for shares created a class of superrich oligarchs by allowing them to acquire the nation's assets at almost no cost. The scheme, however, provided very little in badly needed revenue to the government. In 1995, for example, the mortgage auctions of twenty-one of Russia's most profitable enterprises—the crown jewels of the Soviet economy—netted a total revenue of just $691.4 million and 400 billion rubles, a fraction of their real value.[15]

By April 1996, the oligarchs were a well-established institution in Russia, and even though they owed almost all their wealth to theft, they presented themselves as enterprising capitalists with an indisputable right to rule. A letter signed by thirteen oligarchs and published in leading Russian newspapers issued a veiled threat that appeared to be directed against the communists, who were gaining in the public opinion polls. "Those who rely on social confrontation and ideological revanchism," the letter said, "should understand that the national entrepreneurs have the necessary resources and will to deal with . . . unprincipled . . . politicians."[16]

The pillaging of the country led to economic collapse. In the period 1992–98, Russia's gross domestic product fell by half. (During the Great Depression, the American economy shrank by 30.5 percent.) The collapse of industrial production was even greater, declining 56 percent between 1992 and 1998—a worse fall than under German occupation during World War II.[17] Russia became a classic third world country, selling raw materials to import consumer goods. People went months and even years without being paid. Millions were forced to spend weekends in the countryside, growing their own food in order to survive.

The economic disaster was accompanied by a demographic catastrophe. Between 1990 and 1994, male life expectancy fell by more than six years.[18] By 1998 it was fifty-seven years, the lowest in the industrial world.[19] The almost vertical rise in the death rate was nearly unprecedented for a country that was not at war, and at first, Western demographers did not believe the figures. During the 1990s, the Russian population fell by 750,000 a year.[20]

The government, having received very little from privatization, regularly spent more than it had. In a bid to narrow the deficit, it began issuing short-term government obligations (GKOs). These were denominated in rubles and usually had a three- to six-month term. The market in GKOs grew from $3 billion at the end of 1994 to $42.7 billion in 1996 and $64.7 billion in 1997.[21] But as the government's financial position worsened, the interest rate rose, sometimes reaching 160 percent. By mid-1998, the government was spending $1 billion a week simply to meet its obligations.[22] Faced with an overwhelming financial crisis, on August 17 the government devalued the currency, defaulted on $40 billion worth of treasury bills, and halted the repayment of commercial debt. Prices rose sharply and the nascent middle class was destroyed.

The 1998 collapse was a shock for Russian society. People returned from summer vacations to find that the cash machines of their banks were locked. Currency exchange points posted new ruble-dollar exchange rates every hour. People began to scoop up everything in the stores, including salt, sugar, matches, and flour. Many small businesses collapsed, and there was a rash of contract killings of borrowers who could not repay their debts. Living standards fell by an estimated 40 percent. Many had hoped that the economy was getting better, but it now seemed to have irrevocably collapsed. Yeltsin's approval rating fell to low single digits, and his disapproval reached 80 percent.[23] This, in turn, created extreme uneasiness among the oligarchs and others who made fortunes during the 1990s, and brought on the succession crisis that led to the bombing of the Russian apartment buildings in 1999.

The third process that created Russia's oligarchy was criminalization. Like privatization, the modern era of criminalization in Russia began during perestroika. The Gorbachev era reforms started with the legalization of "cooperatives," which became the only privately run businesses in the Soviet Union. The cooperatives quickly prospered, but because the police protected only state enterprises and it was illegal to hire private guards, gangs sprang up all over the country to extort money from them.

The gangs recruited weightlifters and boxers from sport clubs to serve as enforcers and staked out territory. Anyone operating a business on a gang's "territory" had to pay tribute (*dan*). The gangs, in return, protected their clients from other gangs and became their roof (*krysha*). By 1992, nearly every kiosk and store owner and every trader in the markets was making payoffs to gangsters. In addition to protection, primarily from themselves, the gangs also provided other services. If there was a dispute, businessmen often resolved the matter with the help of their respective kryshas at a meeting (*strelka*). There was usually an attempt to resolve disputes peacefully. But the threat of violence was always present. Gang members usually came to a strelka fully armed.

Most gangs were organized on the basis of an ethnic group or a region; the most important ones developed highly sophisticated structures. They had their own analytical departments, staffed with veterans of the KGB and the police, who were responsible for planning murders and setting up wiretapping, including wiretapping the gang's own members. They were supplied with the latest weapons and equipment from the armed forces. They employed marketing specialists to help identify targets for extortion, and lawyers and accountants to help resolve disputes involving businesses under their "protection."

Initially, the gangs' most lucrative targets, in addition to gas stations and casinos, were markets where transactions were carried out in cash. Many of these had a turnover of billions of dollars in unregistered revenues. According to various estimates, the financial flows of one Moscow market, the Cherkizovskaya, came to $8 billion a year.[24]

As a source of wealth, however, not even the biggest markets could compare to the state budget. When the criminal gangs saw "businessmen" using their connections to acquire vast unearned wealth, they began to use terror to take over the new enterprises. In the early 1990s, hundreds of bankers, businessmen, and government personnel became the victims of contract murders. Thirty-five bankers were murdered in Russia in 1993 alone.[25]

The criminal terror, however, was short-lived. Soon the gangsters, businessmen, and corrupt officials began to work together. The gangsters needed the businessmen because they required places to invest their capital but lacked the expertise to run large enterprises. The businessmen needed the gangsters to enforce contracts and collect debts. (In the early 1990s, many would-be entrepreneurs borrowed money to set up businesses and then forgot to repay it.) And both needed crooked officials to provide licenses and permissions on a noncompetitive basis and to shield them from the law.

The criminals' behavior was typically brutal and aggressive at first, but it improved over time. Many gangsters, wishing to be seen as "businessmen," learned to negotiate and to keep their word. They began buying suits from leading European tailors and patronizing the best Moscow hair stylists. Their identity was betrayed only by their weakness for gold chains and a tendency to lose control and revert to threats when encountering resistance.

For their own safety, Russian businessmen learned which companies were most closely connected to gangsters or were fronts for organized crime. The situation was more complicated for a foreigner doing business in Russia. He frequently found that his dealings with a commercial partner led directly to contact with criminals demanding money for protection or for permission to do business. If he turned to the authorities to defend him, he often found that the criminals seeking to "protect" him had connections going to the very top.

Besides a criminalized economy, the new society developed an authoritarian political system. Yeltsin was lionized for his role in the overthrow of communism, but he quickly demonstrated that he had no understanding of genuine democracy or the separation of powers. The system he sought to create in Russia was designed to serve only his own drive for power.

In October 1993, the two most important branches of government in Russia, the executive branch and the parliament, went to war. The parliament had been Yeltsin's ally. In November 1991, it voted Yeltsin special powers, and after the Soviet Union's collapse, it approved his radical reform program. Yeltsin, however, wanted full control over the economic reform process and was not ready to share power with anyone. This made conflict inevitable.

The first twenty-one months of Yeltsin's postcommunist rule was marked by rising tension between the two branches of government. In January 1992, the sudden removal of price controls unleashed hyperinflation. Yeltsin had forecast lower prices within half a year and economic recovery by the fall. By the end of December, however, prices were rising at a rate of 2,318 percent.[26] Goods appeared in the stores, but 99 percent of the population could not afford them. Many Russians took to the street to sell their belongings. In this situation, the deputies expressed opposition to aspects of the reforms. Yeltsin ignored them. He did not lobby the deputies, and he paid no attention to their debates.

On March 15, 1992, Ruslan Khasbulatov, the speaker of the parliament, demanded the resignation of Yegor Gaidar and his team, whose predictions regarding inflation had proved completely unrealistic. He described the reformers as "inexperienced boys." In June, Khasbulatov and Alexander Rutskoi, the vice president, intensified their attacks on the government. Yeltsin responded by trying to concentrate all decision making in the executive branch, and the Russian government soon had as many bureaucrats and agencies as had existed under the U.S.S.R. Having been supported by two-thirds of the parliament in November 1991, Yeltsin found himself opposed by two-thirds of the deputies six months later.

As the cold weather approached, with about half the population living below the poverty line, the conflict between the two sides intensified. Khasbulatov privately described Yeltsin as a "drunkard" and "mentally ill," and proposals circulated in the government for abolishing parliament.[27] On March 20, 1993, Yeltsin announced that he was signing a decree banning any activities by the parliament that limited the powers of the president. This led the parliament to vote a motion for impeachment. The motion gained a majority but failed for lack of a two-thirds vote. A short time later, a new referendum was set for April 25 on the subjects of trust in the president and his economic policies.

The referendum yielded a strong victory for Yeltsin. It was achieved in part with the help of George Soros, the American financier whose secret contributions to offshore accounts controlled by Anatoly Chubais, the head of privatization, funded a massive advertising campaign that overwhelmed the opposition.[28] Nonetheless, the public support stunned the deputies, who believed that Yeltsin's economic policies were unpopular. Buoyed by the results, Yeltsin continued to rule by decree even though his November 1991 grant of special powers had run out. The parliament sent Yeltsin's decrees to the Constitutional Court, freezing their implementation. Laws and decrees were soon in conflict all over the country.

When, in the summer of 1993, the Supreme Soviet recalculated the budget submitted by Yeltsin, raising pensions and increasing the salaries of teachers, doctors, and others paid out of state funds, the confrontation reached its apogee. The Supreme Soviet's budget provided for a deficit of 28 trillion rubles, or 25 percent of the total national product.[29] The executive branch said that this would wreck the reform process. Yeltsin vowed to ignore it. At the same time, he made preparations to break the parliament's resistance. He visited the bases of army units in the Moscow oblast to shore up support and doubled or tripled the salaries of officers.[30]

In August, Yeltsin and his advisers began working on a decree disbanding parliament. The original proposal called not only for the dissolution of the parliament but for the banning of the Constitutional Court and the subordination of the general prosecutor to the president.[31] In September, Yeltsin and Khasbulatov each invited the other to resign.

Finally, speaking before a meeting of deputies on September 18, Khasbulatov raised the subject of Yeltsin's alcoholism. "It is unacceptable," he said, "when officials give the impression that there is nothing wrong with [drinking]. . . . After all, he drinks, that means he is one of us. But if he is 'one of us' "—at this point Khasbulatov gestured in the direction of the Kremlin and pulled back his third finger with his thumb, snapping it against his throat—"let him occupy himself with peasant work and not government." The gesture and Khasbulatov's remarks were promptly reported to Yeltsin, who decided that the time had come to finish with the parliament once and for all.[32]

On September 21, Yeltsin announced on television that he was issuing decree number 1400, abolishing the Congress of People's Deputies and the Supreme Soviet. He said that elections for new representative organs and a referendum on a new draft constitution would be held December 11–12, 1993.

Shortly after midnight, Khasbulatov opened a meeting of the Supreme Soviet to take up the question of whether Yeltsin's action fell under article 121-6 of the Constitution, which provided for the removal of the president and his replacement by the vice president in the event of an attempt to abolish parliament. The question was put to a vote. The deputies voted 136 in favor and 6 against. This was followed by a vote naming Alexander Rutskoi president. Rutskoi took the oath of office, declared decree 1400 invalid, and said he was taking responsibility for the security of the state. Khasbulatov urged the deputies not to leave the parliament building. Russia now had two heads of state and the beginnings of two separate governments.

In August 1991, Yeltsin had defied the leaders of the pro-communist coup from the same White House where the deputies were now preparing to resist the abolition of the parliament. In 1991, the coup leaders did not shut off the telephones and electricity to Yeltsin and the other members of the Russian government. Yeltsin, however, apparently had no intention of repeating that mistake. He first cut off the interurban telephone lines and then the entire 205 exchange, eliminating phone service for not just the White House but the entire Krasnopresenskaya area. The Moscow city authorities then cut off the building's heat and hot water, and sent large numbers of police to the approaches to the White House.

On September 22, nationalists arrived to defend the White House. The leaders of the parliament, fearful that the building would be easily cleared if it were left undefended, started arming the volunteers. The defenders included members of the Union of Officers, a communist group, the fascist Russian National Unity group, and veterans of ethnic conflicts in Abkhazia and Trans-Dniester. Once armed, they formed units that ceased to be under the control of the deputies. Meanwhile, communist demonstrators rallied on the street in support of the parliament and were beaten by the police.

As preparations for a possible armed confrontation grew, there was increasing support for the parliament in the provinces. By the afternoon of the 22nd, twenty-three regional soviets had voted to support the Supreme Soviet and to treat decree 1400 as invalid on their territory. On September 23, Valery Zorkin, the head of the Constitutional Court, suggested new elections of both the president and the parliament as a way of resolving the crisis. The proposal, which became known as the "zero option," gained popularity but was rejected by Yeltsin and his supporters, ostensibly because this would lead to a power vacuum but actually because acceptance would mean recognizing the existence of the parliament that Yeltsin had just abolished. Yeltsin nonetheless promised that he would not use force against the White House.

At 10:03 PM on September 23, the electricity in the White House was cut off and the already unheated building was plunged into darkness. The deputies lit candles and continued to meet, but there was a change in the psychological atmosphere. In the darkness, the White House's defenders became more important. They set up posts on all landings and staircases and began to check IDs and shine lights in faces. It was now obvious that they intended to answer only to their own commanders. At the same time, false rumors of military and worker support for the deputies led many to expect a popular revolt and inspired continuous radicalization.

On September 28, up to ten thousand demonstrators gathered in front of police roadblocks to support the White House. The police attacked in force, beating people of all ages indiscriminately. Shortly afterward, steps were taken to seal off the White House completely. It was surrounded with barbed wire, and thousands of heavily armed troops cut off access to the part of the city center where it was located. Khasbulatov told the deputies, "The White House has become the first concentration camp of the Yeltsin democratic Gulag."

The next day, Alexei II, the Russian Orthodox patriarch, called for talks, and negotiations began a day later in the Danilovsky

Monastery under Alexei's sponsorship. The presidential side could not refuse to take part in talks called by the patriarch, but the talks were not to Yeltsin's advantage. They implicitly recognized parliament as an equal branch of government, and as they progressed, the pressure on Yeltsin increased. Representatives of regional soviets in Moscow called for an end to the blockade of the White House. In Novosibirsk, representatives of fourteen Siberian oblasts and republics threatened that if Yeltsin did not agree to the "zero option," they would stop paying taxes, cut the trans-Siberian railroad, and announce the creation of an independent Siberian republic.[33]

In this situation, attention focused on the armed defenders of the White House and the communist demonstrators on the street. Yeltsin's promise not to use force against the White House seemed to commit him to a standoff during which his support in the armed forces could weaken while support for the deputies in the regional soviets grew. The extremists, however, were an unpredictable element. If they could be provoked to use violence, Yeltsin could attack the parliament in "self-defense."

On October 3, thousands of communist demonstrators gathered in front of the police lines on the Krymsky Bridge. The police cordon had been set up not in front of the bridge but in the middle, depriving the police of strategic depth. Moreover, there were only two lines of police, which meant that they were vastly outnumbered. For nearly a week, protestors had been beaten by the police, and many of those victims were now in the front line of the demonstrators, armed with bricks and clubs. Suddenly there was a hail of rocks and the marchers threw themselves on the police lines. The line broke; the police fled. The crowd began walking toward the White House. Police were manning a barricade of fire engines and trucks in their path, but as the crowd approached, they also withdrew. The crowd took over nearly twenty trucks, many with the keys in the ignition.

Demonstrators drove the seized trucks to the square behind the White House, with the crowd following. When they arrived, Rutskoi, Khasbulatov, and the rest of the parliamentary leadership emerged on the balcony facing the square. Rutskoi told the demonstrators to take over the Mayoralty, which was next to the White House, and then the Ostankino Television Tower. The crowd and armed defenders of the White House stormed the Mayoralty and seized it. In the parking lot, they found more buses and trucks, also with keys in the ignitions. These vehicles were added to the fleet that now left for the Ostankino Tower, with thousands more heading to the tower on foot.

The first buses and trucks arrived at Ostankino at 5:30 PM. Those who had walked arrived later, but by 7 PM, there was a crowd of nearly four thousand in the square.[34] The demonstrators included twenty people with automatic weapons and a grenade launcher taken, along with two grenades, from the OMON riot police. Unknown to the demonstrators, however, inside the building were five hundred police and military armed with 320 automatic weapons. Reinforcements would later swell their number to nine hundred.[35]

The protestors' intention was to give the parliamentary side access to the airwaves, which had been dominated by pro-Yeltsin propaganda. General Albert Makashov, the leader of the White House defense, who arrived at Ostankino with a group of armed fighters, demanded that the guards open the doors. In the event of a refusal, he threatened to storm the building. A young man began preparing the grenade launcher while the troops inside the building positioned themselves behind concrete parapets on the first floor.

At that moment, two trucks of the pro-parliament forces crashed into the entrance to the television tower and the plate glass windows next to it. This was followed by a powerful explosion at the entrance as the grenade launcher was fired at the door, and by another explosion inside the building. It was the latter explosion that killed Nikolai Sitnikov, a member of the Interior Forces Vytyas unit.

Suddenly, a solid sheet of fire from inside the building raked the demonstrators in the square. Most of the armed fascists were shielded by a roof over the entryway, but the unarmed protestors, onlookers, and journalists were hit by a torrent of orange-yellow tracer bullets. The square was quickly littered with the bodies of the wounded and dead. As the wounded called out, "Don't shoot" and "Please, help us," their bodies were repeatedly riddled with automatic weapons fire. Civilians dived for cover as the troops fired at anyone who lifted his head.

The American lawyer Terry Michael Duncan, who had already pulled three people to safety, went to the aid of Otto Pohl, a photo correspondent for the *New York Times* who was shot in the stomach after shouting to the troops that he was a foreign correspondent. The troops did not allow anyone else to approach them. As Duncan tried to encourage Pohl to stay conscious, he was also shot. Several Russians risked their lives to pull Pohl to safety. One of them, Yuri Mikhailov, a thirty-five-year-old Moscow resident, called to the soldiers and asked if he could rescue Duncan. This was met with a burst of profanity. Mikhailov nonetheless tried. He was shot in the back and killed. The firing then intensified and Duncan was shot in the head.[36]

The supporters of the parliament did not return fire. Nonetheless, Russian television announced that Ostankino had been seized by an armed mob. At 8:45 PM, Gaidar appeared on television and called on Muscovites to take to the streets to show support for the president. Yeltsin also released a statement, saying that the street battles were a "calculated action, planned in advance by the former leaders of the parliament."[37] He declared a state of emergency. At a meeting in the ministry of defense, the commanders of the military districts announced their support for Yeltsin.

By 9 PM, euphoria in the White House over the apparent easy victory had given way to horror as deputies returned from Ostankino in shock. Ilya Konstantinov told the other deputies, "It's bloody kasha." Oleg Plotnikov, a deputy from the moderate Smena faction, said, "I've never seen so many corpses in my life."[38]

In the early morning hours, Yeltsin went to the ministry of defense and persuaded defense minister Pavel Grachev to order the storming of the White House. The attack began at 6:55 AM. Internal troops shot defenders of the White House, including teenagers who were outside the building. At 8 AM they opened fire on the building itself, shattering rows of windows. In response to defensive fire from the White House, the attackers directed large-caliber machine guns and tank artillery at the twelfth and thirteenth floors, which were quickly consumed in flames. Those inside the White House—including deputies, journalists, and employees—fled to the safest place in the building: the hall of the Council of Nationalities, which was designed as a bomb shelter.

The shooting continued with great intensity. As the hours passed, however, the return fire grew weak. Tanks on the Novy Arbat Bridge blew out sections of the deserted upper floors. Finally, with resistance having all but ceased, members of the Alpha antiterrorist unit entered the building and accepted the deputies' surrender.

According to official figures, 123 people were killed and 384 wounded in the two-day civil war. Of these, 46 were killed at Ostankino and 124 were wounded.[39] But there is doubt about these figures. The government originally refused to report the number killed, which led to reports that it was as high as 1,500.[40] A report on Ukrainian radio put the number killed at 2,783.[41]

Whatever the true death toll, I became convinced that Yeltsin owed his victory to a provocation. For days before the events of October 3–4, the center of Moscow was sealed off by thousands of riot troops and police. Yet on October 3, after the demonstrators broke through the police lines on the Krymsky Bridge, the police had all but disappeared. The police abandoned one checkpoint after another, leaving behind trucks and buses with keys in the ignition. The demonstrators were able to take over the Mayoralty and proceed to the Ostankino Television Tower without hindrance. When they arrived at Ostankino, Makashov and his twenty or so fighters organized a meeting and began issuing ultimatums, but they had no chance of taking the building.

When a grenade exploded in the entrance to Ostankino, the internal troops opened fire not on the armed attackers but on the unarmed crowd in the square. The fact that the troops deliberately killed those who were wounded and fired on ambulances that were rushing to their aid[42] suggests that those behind the attack intended to kill as many people as possible. The conflict at Ostankino was used to persuade the army to attack the White House. It is possible that a high death toll, which could be blamed on the demonstrators, helped make the case for intervention.

An investigation into the October events by a team from the office of the general prosecutor rapidly uncovered inconsistencies in the story presented by the presidential side. The deaths of Sitnikov and of Sergei Krasilnikov, a video editor in Ostankino, were used by the presidential side to justify the order to attack the demonstrators. The investigation, however, showed that neither of these killings was the responsibility of the pro-parliamentary forces. Sitnikov died not from grenade fire by the pro-parliament forces but from the explosion of a device inside the building. The shot that killed Krasilnikov was fired in a corridor full of Interior Ministry troops. It could not have come from outside the building.[43]

When it became clear that the investigators were uncovering evidence implicating the presidential side, Yeltsin agreed to an amnesty for the leaders of parliament, whom he had earlier described as "bandits and criminals." They were released from prison, and the investigation of Yeltsin's own actions came to a halt.

After his victory in the October confrontation, Yeltsin presented the country with a new draft constitution that gave the president near-dictatorial powers. Under the proposed constitution, the Supreme Soviet would be replaced with a smaller body, the State Duma, which would have virtually no control over the executive branch. The president would have the power to appoint without interference all ministers except the prime minister, who would have to be confirmed by the Duma. If the Duma rejected three of his candidates for prime minister, the president would be able to dissolve the Duma. The president would have control over the budget and appoint the director of the Central Bank and the justices of the Constitutional Court. Removing the president would require a two-thirds majority of the parliament as well as approval by the Supreme Court and the Constitutional Court. Laws would be passed by the Duma, but they could be vetoed by the president, and the veto could be overridden only by a two-thirds vote of the Duma, a near impossibility in a parliament expected to contain numerous factions.

The draft constitution was put to a vote simultaneously with elections to the new parliament on December 12, 1993, only a month after the publication of the text. In the referendum, 54.4 percent of eligible voters were said to have participated, with 58.4 percent voting for and 41.6 percent against the new constitution.[44] The constitution was thus supported by about 30 percent of the electorate. Technically this was enough: Yeltsin had established a rule whereby only 25 percent of eligible voters had to vote yes for the constitution to become law.[45] There were immediate suspicions, however, that the approval was fraudulent. Particular concern was focused on the appearance of nearly nine million unexplained ballots.[46] An independent analysis by Alexander Sobyanin of the pro-government Russia's Choice Party showed that only 46.1 percent of the electorate had voted, not the 54.4 percent the government claimed, in which case the turnout was 3.9 percent short of the required minimum. The presidential team never explained the origin of the extra ballots and ignored all demands for an investigation. It is highly likely that the 1993 Constitution was never approved by the population.[47]

Yeltsin's destruction of the Supreme Soviet and the creation of a superpresidency destroyed any possibility in Russia of a genuine separation of powers. The first serious consequence was the war in Chechnya. Yeltsin needed a war because since the events of October 1993, he could no longer blame the parliament for his failures. Oleg Lobov, the secretary of Yeltsin's Security Council, told Sergei Yushenkov, the chairman of the Duma Defense Committee, that a war in Chechnya was coming. "On the telephone," Yushenkov told the journalists Carlotta Gall and Thomas de Waal, "Lobov used the phrase that: 'It is not only a question of the integrity of Russia. We need a small, victorious war to raise the President's ratings.' "[48] A force of volunteers opposed to the separatist regime in Chechnya was assembled by the Russian security services to seize Grozny, the Chechen capital, and set up a puppet government that would request the introduction of Russian troops. But on November 26, 1994, the volunteers were routed by Chechen troops loyal to Djofar Dudayev, the Chechen leader. Yeltsin ordered the Chechens to lay down their arms by December 15. Despite the deadline, the Russian military began air strikes on December 2, and on the 11th, three columns of Russian army units moved into Chechnya.

Democrats, including Gaidar, who had supported Yeltsin's suppression of the parliament, now found that giving unchecked power to Yeltsin came at a price. He had unilaterally committed the army to a war against Russian citizens on Russia's own territory.

The destruction of the Supreme Soviet also assured Yeltsin an apparently undeserved second term in office. After the parliament was disbanded by force, the communists were apparently too intimidated to seriously contest an election. Yeltsin was believed to have won the 1996 presidential election, albeit with the help of massive violations of the campaign financing rules. But in February 2012, at a meeting with four members of the opposition, President Dmitri Medvedev said that this was not the case. When the four protested the falsification of the results of the previous December's parliamentary elections, Medvedev indicated that falsification is not unusual: "There is hardly any doubt who won [the 1996 presidential election]. It was not Boris Nikolaevich Yeltsin."[49]

Viktor Ilyukhin, a communist who in 1996 was the head of the Duma Security Committee, said in an interview with the site Gazeta. ru that Zyuganov did not protest the theft of the election because in light of the events in October 1993, he was afraid of triggering a civil war. "The Yeltsin entourage was ready to use force in the event of a victory by Zyuganov," Ilyukhin said. "They did not hesitate to say to us, 'We will not simply hand over power.'" There were fifty thousand armed guards in Moscow, many of them Afghan veterans who were on Yeltsin's side, and "This force could have been used and that was more terrible than an open confrontation. When tanks move, they are visible but this could be used to attack from behind. At the same time, besides the Alpha unit, Yeltsin was creating more specialized military units."[50] According to Ilyukhin, declaring the elections falsified would have meant calling people into the streets, and this could have caused the communist leaders to be arrested or killed.[51]

Anatoly Chubais, who was Yeltsin's campaign manager at the time, said that "of course" there were violations in the campaign, but if the 1996 vote were to be dismissed as a fraud, "then we automatically have to deem both of President Putin's terms illegitimate along with the presidency of Medvedev. . . . There would be nothing left of Russia's post-Soviet history."[52]

By July 1996, when Yeltsin began his second term as president, parliament's role was so reduced that Yeltsin was able to rule effectively alone. Ironically, it was then that his health began to fail, making him unable to wield the power he had taken such pains to accumulate. He surrendered authority to his daughter, Tatyana Dyachenko, and Valentin Yumashev, the journalist who in the 1980s had helped him write his first volume of memoirs. Dyachenko began to be called the "true ruler of Russia." She in turn relied on Berezovsky, who, according to a commentary in *Moskovsky Komsomolets*, "became the chief cash disburser, sponsor, and financial director of Yeltsin's tightly knit family."[53]

Dyachenko and Berezovsky were highly corrupt and therefore vulnerable to criminal prosecution in the event that Yeltsin's successor as president was not reliable. It was this dilemma, imposed by Yeltsin's drive to monopolize power, that made it necessary to ensure that he was succeeded by someone who would not hold him and his family accountable for their abuse of power. The result was "Operation Successor," which led directly to the apartment bombings and Russia's final transition from a failing democracy to a full-fledged dictatorship.

In 1998, in the wake of the Russian financial crisis, Yeltsin nominated Yevgeny Primakov, the former head of the Foreign Intelligence Service, to be prime minister. The crisis had destroyed much of Yeltsin's remaining support, and the appointment of Primakov was a compromise with the political opposition after the Duma twice voted down Yeltsin's attempt to reappoint former prime minister Viktor Chernomyrdin to the post. Primakov, however, was not content with the political status quo. Once appointed, he authorized an investigation of the Yeltsin family and some of the oligarchs, starting with Berezovsky.

In the fall of 1997, Carla del Ponte, the Swiss prosecutor general, was given police reports showing that Russian organized crime controlled more than three hundred firms in Switzerland and that a Swiss businessman of Albanian origin, Behgjet Pacolli, who headed Mabetex, a construction company that was doing reconstruction work on the Kremlin, was providing unexplained funds to Yeltsin and his daughters. These documents were forwarded to Yuri Skuratov, the Russian general prosecutor, in September 1998. On January 22, 1999, a raid on the Mabetex office in Lugano turned up records showing payments of $600,000 on the credit cards of Yeltsin's daughters. Pacolli also seemed to have paid kickbacks to Pavel Borodin, the director of the presidential administration, for the contracts to work on the Kremlin. Skuratov, meanwhile, intensified his investigation into Berezovsky's activities. On February 2 and 4, heavily armed FSB agents raided Aeroflot and the private security firm Atoll, which was also associated with Berezovsky.[54]

The investigation of Dyachenko and Berezovsky was a direct challenge to the regime. It came, moreover, at a time when Yeltsin was reportedly suffering blackouts and periods of disorientation, and many important decisions were reportedly being made by Dyachenko.

The Yeltsin entourage was not slow to react to the efforts of Skuratov, who, with Primakov's blessing, was seriously investigating them. The FSB, under its director at the time, Vladimir Putin, secretly filmed Skuratov in a sauna having sex with two prostitutes. The film was shown on the state television channel, RTR, and Skuratov was forced to resign. An arrest order against Berezovsky was revoked.

Eliminating Skuratov, however, could not eliminate the long-term threat to the Yeltsin family in the event of a future loss of power. Yeltsin increasingly appeared confused and remote. He took no role in either the daily political struggle or the running of the economy. His aides decided that he was more suited to the role of guarantor of the Constitution. But Yeltsin handled even this role poorly, avoiding decisions and limiting himself to generalities.

Sensing Yeltsin's weakness, the opposition in the State Duma scheduled an impeachment vote. On May 12, the day before the opening of the hearings, Yeltsin fired Primakov and installed the interior minister, Sergei Stepashin, as acting premier. Yeltsin's readiness to fire Primakov, the most popular politician in the country, was taken as a signal to the deputies that in the event of impeachment, he was ready to suppress the parliament by force. There were five charges against Yeltsin: that he had illegally broken up the Soviet Union, that he had illegally dispersed the Supreme Soviet, that he had violated the Constitution in starting the war in Chechnya, that he had weakened the Russian armed forces, and that his reform policies had contributed to the genocide of the Russian people. Of the five charges, only the one concerning the war in Chechnya had a good chance of gaining the two-thirds vote necessary for impeachment. Accordingly, Kremlin agents circulated through the State Duma, bribing deputies not to vote for impeachment on this count. They even offered to pay deputies who voted for impeachment on other counts if they would refrain from supporting it on this count. In the end, the vote on Chechnya showed 283 in favor of impeachment, 17 votes short of the necessary two-thirds. The other counts received even fewer votes. After the totals were announced, Zyuganov told reporters, "This was all bought."

With the failure of the impeachment motion, Luzhkov began to organize the opposition to Yeltsin in anticipation of the 2000 elections. He recruited Primakov for his Fatherland–All Russia movement and said that if Primakov chose to run for president, he would stand aside and support him. At first, Yeltsin's allies hoped that Stepashin would be able to defeat Primakov in an election. It soon became clear, however, that Stepashin was unenthusiastic about attacking Primakov and Luzhkov, and there were reports that he rejected schemes for introducing a state of emergency and canceling the presidential elections out of fear of igniting a civil war. *Moscow News* reported that one of the schemes discussed among insiders, known as "Storm in Moscow," called for acts of terror in Moscow. On August 5, however, a Chechen Islamist force invaded Dagestan. On August 9, Stepashin was dismissed and Putin was named prime minister, and between September 4 and 16, Russia was wracked by the apartment bombings that completely changed the course of political events.

The shock of the bombings allowed Putin, with the help of state television, to project the image of a tough leader avenging an attack on innocent civilians. At noon on December 31, 1999, Yeltsin announced in a televised address that he was resigning three months early as president. In the early afternoon, Vladimir Putin was appointed acting president at a Kremlin ceremony. His first act was to issue a decree granting Yeltsin immunity from prosecution. The decree shielded Yeltsin from searches, arrest, and interrogation and protected his cars, telephone calls, documents, luggage, and correspondence.

The elections were set for March 26. Putin eschewed serious campaigning and avoided even explaining where he stood on the issues facing the country. He won with 54 percent of the vote. The runner-up, communist leader Gennady Zyuganov, got 30 percent. The Russian people had elected someone about whom they knew nothing except that he was avenging the apartment bombings.

The rise of a criminal oligarchy and the reliance on violent and illegal methods to create an authoritarian political system inevitably affected the public consciousness. They led to a blurring of moral distinctions, a growth of irrationality, and a disregard for the value of human life. The blurring of moral distinctions was a natural consequence of a transition process that rewarded criminality. Success in Russia was so closely associated with crime that it surprised no one when gangsters became civic leaders. Otari Kvantrishvili, who emerged as one of the capital's leading socialites, began his criminal career in the 1980s, when he organized his own gang to engage in currency speculation, gambling, and extortion of prostitutes working in Moscow's leading hotels. To manage these enterprises, Kvantrishvili founded a holding company, Association Twenty-first Century, which then sought to engage in the export of oil, timber, and nonferrous metals. To gain access to raw materials he needed political contacts. He developed these with the help of Iosif Kobson, a singer with ties to political leaders. Through Kobson, whose title in the organization was "vice president for humanitarian questions," Kvantrishvili established connections to Yeltsin's entourage, former mayor Luzhkov, and high-ranking officials in the FSB and MVD. He also arbitrated criminal disputes and soon became the unofficial emissary of organized crime to society and society's representative to the criminal world.[55]

Association Twenty-first Century became known as an organization that could help people "solve problems." Criminals turned to Kvantrishvili for help with the authorities, and businessmen turned to him for help with the gangs. To bolster his respectability, Kvantrishvili organized the Yashin Fund for the Social Defense of Sportsmen. This turned him into a Moscow celebrity. He was invited on television to discuss the living conditions of athletes, and he became a frequent guest at beauty pageants, sporting events, and celebrity parties. At the end of 1993 he decided to enter politics and created his own political party, Sportsmen of Russia. On April 5, 1994, however, he was shot by a sniper as he left a bathhouse surrounded by bodyguards. The crowd at his funeral consisted equally of members of the political and cultural elite and organized crime leaders. Among those attending were Luzhkov, Gusinsky, Shamil Tarpishchev, Yeltsin's tennis coach, and Alexander Rosenbaum, a popular singer. As Kvantrishvili was laid to rest, Rosenbaum said, "the country has lost—I'm not afraid of this word—a leader."[56]

Another leader was Anatoly Bykov, whose organized crime group took over the Krasnoyarsk Aluminum Factory (KRAZ) in one of the bloodiest episodes in the history of Russian privatization. Bykov was implicated in the killings of Krasnoyarsk's criminal leaders and of businessmen who had paid protection money to the recently deceased criminal authorities and did not want to pay Bykov as well. In late July and early August 1994, five leading Krasnoyarsk businessmen were killed in ten days. Dozens of killings followed. The victims included government officials, businessmen, and Mustaf Mustafin, who had arrived from Moscow to force Bykov to give money to the all-Russian criminal treasury (*obshchak*). Also killed were assassins sent to kill Bykov and four businessmen whom Bykov mistook for hired killers. Bykov's gunmen not only mowed down their victims in full public view, they also shot anyone who got in the way. While running for a seat on the Krasnoyarsk Krai Legislative Assembly, Bykov acknowledged that he had taken "some illegal chances" but said he had broken the law only to establish order and rid the region of criminals. He was elected with 80 percent of the vote.[57]

One of Russia's most ruthless criminals was Alexander Solonik ("Sasha Makedonsky"), a professional killer famous for, among other things, being able to fire accurately and at the same time from pistols in both hands. Solonik became the boyfriend of one of Russia's most glamorous women, Svetlana Kotova, a former Miss Russia. They met in a Moscow nightclub on New Year's Eve, 1997, and Kotova traveled to Greece on January 25 at his invitation. She was met at the plane with armloads of flowers and taken to Solonik's villa in a chauffeur-driven Mercedes. She told her mother by phone that what she was living was not life but a miracle. The miracle ended on January 30, when gangsters from the Kurgan criminal organization arrived at the villa. While they were talking to Solonik, someone threw a thin cord around his neck and strangled him from behind. Members of the group then found Svetlana on the second floor, where they strangled her to eliminate a possible witness.[58]

The Yeltsin years were also a time of widespread faith in mysticism and the paranormal. Without the discredited communist ideology to make sense of what was happening around them, people turned to witches, sorcerers, and fortune-tellers.

In the early 1990s, Russia's most popular public personality was Anatoly Kashpirovsky, a psychiatrist and trained hypnotist who conducted televised healing sessions in which he treated everything from high blood pressure and hip injuries to emotional distress. Dressed entirely in black, he spoke in a voice that observers described as both "reassuring and oddly threatening,"[59] which he used to lull the television audience into a trance. At his live appearances, crowds writhed and sobbed at his command, thinking they were experiencing the casting out of devils. Also popular was Allan Chumak, a former journalist with flowing white hair, who after a brief introduction slowly moved his hands across the television screen, supposedly charging with healing energy the saucepans full of water that millions of people had placed in front of their sets. Chumak cured various ills. The first part of a day's séance might be for allergies. Those with stomach problems were told to tune in later.[60]

Occult services became a huge business in Russia. Wives appealed to witches to help return their husbands or cast the evil eye on their rivals. Sometimes a client asked a witch to change the behavior of her partner. To achieve this, the witch used a photograph to make a wax figure of the person whose behavior was to be changed, inserted a needle into the figure's sexual parts, and then removed it.[61] Businessmen consulted sorcerers before making decisions, to identify enemies, to predict the results of upcoming cases, and to select targets for contract killings. Instead of resisting these tendencies, the Russian Orthodox Church itself became a kind of cult, with priests blessing businesses, banks, homes, automobiles, and even a tank, and exorcising "unclean powers" for a fee.[62]

Among the many religious groups active in Russia was the Japanese doomsday sect Aum Shinrikyo, which taught that the world was going to end in 1997 and only members of the sect would be saved.

Aum Shinrikyo's leaders established contact with high Russian officials, including Oleg Lobov, the secretary of the Security Council. With his help, members of the sect trained at Russian military bases and shopped for advanced weapons.[63] The sect's activities were forbidden after some of its members launched a sarin gas attack on the Tokyo metro that killed twelve people and injured more than five thousand. At that time, according to some accounts, Aum Shinrikyo had eight times more followers in Russia than in Japan.[64]

Finally, Russia experienced a drastic devaluing of the worth of human life, even by comparison with the Soviet period. In the 1990s, the number of murders reached forty thousand a year, three times as many as in 1990. Compared to an Englishman, a Russian was five times as likely to die in a traffic accident, twenty-five times as likely to accidentally poison himself, seven times as likely to commit suicide, and fifty-four times as likely to be murdered.[65]

I had a chilling encounter with this emerging attitude toward human life while living in Moscow in 1992. One night in October, I left my apartment in the Kolomensky district in Moscow to go for a walk. The approach of winter was already palpable in the early darkness. I walked past the impromptu market near the metro station where Russians were selling their possessions, the booths where Georgians displaced by the war in Abkhazia were cooking *khachapuris,* and the kiosks reinforced with iron bars where the owners sold cigarettes, vodka, and Snickers bars through a small window located well below eye level, forcing the customer to bend over to talk to them.

Russia had never had many automobiles, but now there was traffic on Andropov Prospect and a lot of foreign cars. I turned down Sudostroitelnaya Street, walked past rows of concrete panel apartment blocks, and stopped at a metal notice board full of notes from people seeking accommodation or proposing an exchange. One of the handwritten announcements read: "Are you ill and alone? We are ready to help." It proposed lifetime care for single persons in difficulty in return for legal ownership of their apartment. The note did not include the name or address of an organization, only a phone number. It included a promise to handle legal formalities and said that many people in the area were already being helped.

I stood for a long time in the biting wind, studying the announcement. With the fall of communism, state apartments could now be privatized and become the property of their occupant. The area was full of people who lived alone. This was the first time I was exposed to the apartment racket, but I felt intuitively that anyone who agreed to this arrangement was signing his death warrant. I soon learned that my suspicions were not unfounded. The bodies of those who agreed were discovered by the hundreds, perhaps thousands, in forests and garbage dumps all over Russia.

The Russian government's concern for human life was hardly better. Russian citizens during the Yeltsin years experienced the trauma of losing an entire worldview that had given meaning, however falsely, to their lives. In response, the government removed all restrictions on the sale of alcohol. The result was that at a time when the purchasing power of the average Russian was cut in half, his salary in relation to the cost of vodka increased threefold. The era of cheap vodka and the resulting tranquilization of the population lowered resistance to the pillaging of the country, but at a severe cost to the nation's health.[66]

At the same time, the government failed to finance the system of public health. For the first time, Russians had to pay for many medical services, from necessary medicines to lifesaving operations, and the inability to pay led many to give up on their own lives. By various estimates, five to six million people died prematurely during the Yeltsin period.[67] Igor Gundarov, the head of Russia's State Center for Prophylactic Medicine, saw in the 1990s in Russia an attempt to "transplant souls," to "replace the old, nonmarket soul with a new pragmatic businesslike approach to life. The change was unaccompanied by an effort to provide . . . a reason for which this change should be undertaken. For many people who needed something to live for, this change was intolerable and they lost the will to live because life no longer had any meaning."[68]

Yeltsin was given a chance granted to very few. He was Russia's overwhelmingly popular head of state at a pivotal moment in the country's history after the fall of the Soviet Union and could have helped Russia to break once and for all with its totalitarian past. Unfortunately, he understood communism as an economic phenomenon and assumed that to produce democracy it was necessary only to change economic structures. In fact, communism, which promoted "class values," was always a moral phenomenon whose failings could be addressed only through restoration of the universal values that the communist system denied. This meant, in the first place, establishment of the rule of law. By concentrating on introducing capitalism and carrying out the transition so lawlessly, Yeltsin assured that Russia would be taken over by criminals and that Russian oppression would not end but only enter a new phase.

When Yeltsin handed over power to Vladimir Putin, he said, "take care of Russia." The country, exhausted and demoralized, had no sympathy for the departing Yeltsin. But it welcomed Putin in the hope that his elections marked the start of something new.

# 3

# The Power Vertical

After the devastation wrought by the Yeltsin era, almost any new leader was likely to be perceived as a potential savior. Russians saw in Putin what they wanted him to be, rather than what he was. He also took power at a moment when the Russian economy started to expand.

Although Putin declined to debate in the presidential election campaign, his vow to destroy the terrorists who carried out the apartment bombings resonated with the public. At the same time, a public relations campaign on state-run television helped turn him into a popular hero. He was shown dressed as a fighter pilot, swimming in a river, shooting a Siberian tiger with a sedation dart, and, after a suspicious explosion on August 8 in Moscow's Pushkin Square underpass that killed thirteen people, calming Russians' nerves by tagging a polar bear.

Putin's intention, however, was to create a system in which the regime exercised total power. In his inaugural address May 7, 2000, he said that "the head of the government was always and will always be the person who answers for everything." In fact, even under the 1993 Constitution, which created the superpresidency, the president did not answer for everything. Parliament was responsible for making laws, and the courts for the administration of justice. Putin said that he would be guided "only by the interests of the state." This too was a departure, because Russia is ostensibly a democracy in which the government answers to the people. The promise to be guided only by the interests of the state was implicitly a claim to one-man rule. On foreign policy, Putin said it was important to defend Russian citizens both in Russia and "beyond its boundaries." These words were little noticed at the time, and Russia was still too weak to contemplate foreign aggression, but they were a claim for the future.

Putin did not refer in his speech to individual rights, but his attitude on the subject became clear three months later. On August 12, two massive explosions occurred on board the nuclear submarine *Kursk* during a training exercise, and it sank to the bottom of the Barents Sea. Most of the 118 crew members were killed instantly, but 23 survivors managed to flee to a rear compartment, where they tapped out desperate calls for help on the submarine's hull. The entire world was transfixed by the drama of the trapped Russian sailors, but for four days, the government, unwilling to admit weakness, refused offers of foreign help. Putin only relented in the face of worldwide outrage. The first Norwegian rescuers reached the *Kursk* on August 20. By that time it was too late. The ship was flooded and the entire crew was dead.[1]

Later, when asked by Larry King on CNN what happened to the *Kursk,* Putin said only "It sank," giving an eerie smile.[2] The Russian media called the smile a serious political mistake. In fact, it had few political consequences. But it was an ominous sign of the indifference to suffering that would be a hallmark of the years ahead.

In the system created under Putin, power was exercised through a bureaucracy that answered only to the country's leader. Lies and manipulation helped reconcile the population to this state of affairs, but the regime nonetheless viewed the Russian people with suspicion, rightly regarding their desire for rights as its most dangerous potential threat.

The criminality of the Yeltsin period engendered a hunger for order, which, in the absence of moral content, led to banditry in the guise of a state. A façade of rational government was preserved, but all normal values were displaced. Under optimal conditions, such a structure could rule successfully for a long time. But it was based on the proposition that the good luck would never run out.

The creation and consolidation of the Putin-era system involved installing a vertical chain of command and eliminating alternative centers of power. These processes reinforced each other. An autocratic system was created almost before the population understood what had taken place.

Putin filled the highest posts with those who had worked with him in the St. Petersburg city government or the Leningrad KGB. These included Dmitri Medvedev, chief of staff (and later president); Igor Sechin, deputy chief of staff; Viktor Ivanov, deputy head of the presidential administration; Sergei Ivanov, secretary of the Security Council; and Nikolai Patrushev, head of the FSB. Other posts were filled with veterans of the KGB-FSB and the Interior Ministry. By 2004, the top ministers, half of the Security Council, and 70 percent of the senior regional officials in Russia came from the security services.[3]

Putin's emphasis on his personal cronies and the security services created a distinct atmosphere in the Russian leadership. Like most Soviet citizens, many of Russia's leaders grew up in poverty, living, as Putin did, in communal apartments with shared kitchens and baths. With no reason for success except Putin's patronage, they acquired wealth beyond the dreams of avarice, and repaid the favor with total conformity. Boris Gryzlov, the former speaker of the Duma, once said that if Putin told him to jump out of a window, he would do it.[4] Those officials with security backgrounds also brought the mentality of the KGB: a predilection for spymania and the pursuit of phantoms, alongside a tendency to see themselves as part of a privileged caste and to treat "outsiders"—both ordinary Russians and the West—as enemies.

Andrei Illarionov, who was Putin's economic adviser for his first five years in office, said in testimony before the U.S. Congress that the leadership operates on the basis of mutual support and *omerta*, the Mafia code of silence. It preserves "traditions, hierarchies, codes and habits of [the] secret police. . . . Its members show a high degree of obedience to the current leadership, strong loyalty to each other, rather strict discipline. There are both formal and informal means of enforcing these norms. Violators of the code of conduct are subject to the harshest forms of punishment, including the highest form."[5]

The creation of a "power vertical" emanating from the Kremlin was made possible by a dramatic reversal in Russia's economic fortunes. Russian national income fell by almost half during the 1990s, but sharp rises in world energy prices, coupled with the first benefits of the capitalist economic transformation under Yeltsin and huge pent-up demand, led, under Putin, to an unprecedented economic boom. In 2000, Russia's GDP rose 7.6 percent and industrial production by 9.2 percent. These were the highest growth rates since 1973.[6] The government began to honor its debts. Salaries and pensions were paid and repeatedly raised. Russians who inherited their Soviet era apartments suddenly found that they had disposable cash, and there was a boom in consumption. Shopping malls opened all over the country. Russians rushed to buy cell phones, computers, and cars.

The oil and gas revenue made it possible to organize, equip, and staff government agencies that had been barely functioning, resulting in a semblance of order. Previously, collection of taxes had been chaotic. No one paid personal income tax; few even knew how to pay it. Of five million people who declared their income to the tax authorities in 2000, only fifty thousand admitted to earning more than $30,000.[7] Under Putin, enforcement was organized and taxes began to be collected.

Other government agencies also began to perform their required functions. The strengthening of state institutions, however, did not lead to greater legality. Instead of stamping out criminality, the government apparatus took it over. Anarchy and lack of governance were replaced by meddling and ubiquitous bribe taking. Between 2001 and 2005, according to the INDEM think tank,[8] bribes extorted by the authorities increased nearly tenfold, to over $316 billion. In 2001, Russia ranked 79th in the global Corruption Perceptions Index compiled by Transparency International. By 2006, it was 121st, at the same level as Rwanda.

Besides creating a system of top-down control, Putin acted to eliminate independent centers of power. One by one, institutions capable of providing an alternative to unitary power were subordinated, starting with the media, followed by business, and ending with parliament and the courts. The result was a society in which the regime was the only center of power, drastically limiting the freedom of the population.

"People are disgusted by the inability to function properly," said Elena Panfilova, the Moscow head of Transparency International, in a 2011 interview. "Everyone feels slightly handicapped. You cannot do what you want, invest where you want, say what you want. It creates an uncomfortable atmosphere for life. Everywhere there is the need for political protection and the necessity of being subject to control. The more capable a person, the more he chafes under the restrictions."[9]

Putin had seen the role of television in sabotaging Primakov's presidential candidacy and creating his own favorable image, and he wanted to make sure that the national television stations in particular were always under his control. The first target was NTV, which on the eve of the April 2000 elections had angered the FSB with its investigation into the apartment bombings. On May 11, the headquarters of Media Most, the holding company that owned NTV, was raided by masked men who identified themselves as the tax police. In June, Media Most's chairman, Vladimir Gusinsky, was called to the prosecutor for questioning, supposedly about the origin of several bullets for a decorative pistol that were confiscated in the May 11 raid. That evening he was arrested in connection with the privatization of a St. Petersburg television company, Russian Video, and taken to the Byutyrsky Prison.

On July 16, Gusinsky was charged with fraud and released on the condition that he not leave Moscow. Negotiations then began between Gusinsky and the authorities over the future of NTV. He was offered $300 million and forgiveness of a debt of $473 million to Gazprom in return for Media-Most and NTV, his entire empire. The station alone was valued at more than $1 billion. Faced with the alternative of prison, Gusinsky agreed to the "offer." On July 27, the charges against him were dropped and he left Russia.[10]

With Gusinsky's removal, the type of critical reports that had distinguished NTV in the 1990s disappeared. There were no further programs about the apartment bombings.[11] Instead, NTV concentrated on entertainment, including foreign soap operas and such programs as *Fear Factor*, which rewarded contestants for climbing high buildings, sitting in cells underwater, or eating worms or cockroaches.

The neutralization of NTV was followed by the takeover of ORT (Channel One), the most important television station, which was run by Boris Berezovsky. ORT had supported Putin during the presidential campaign, but once Putin was elected, Berezovsky began to oppose some of his policies, in particular the creation of presidential envoys who could interfere with the ability of governors to make decisions concerning industries in which Berezovsky had an economic interest.

When the *Kursk* sank, ORT went into opposition. The station showed scenes of Putin jet skiing in Sochi and contrasted his behavior with the despair of the doomed sailors' mothers and widows. Putin's popularity rating fell by ten points. ORT's coverage of the *Kursk* disaster is apparently what led Putin to decide to take the station away from Berezovsky. At a meeting in the Kremlin, Alexander Voloshin, Putin's chief of staff, told Berezovsky to give up ORT in two weeks or share the fate of Gusinsky. At a subsequent meeting with Putin, Berezovsky argued that the attacks by ORT actually helped Putin because it showed that he tolerated criticism. Putin responded by accusing Berezovsky of hiring prostitutes to pose as the widows and sisters of the doomed sailors.[12]

Berezovsky left Russia, but Roman Abramovich, his former business partner, met him in western Europe and continued to demand that he give up control of ORT. In December, Berezovsky's friend and collaborator Nikolai Glushkov was arrested. Berezovsky told a Moscow radio station that the arrest was blackmail and that it made no sense for him to struggle further and expose his friends and family to risk. In January, he sold his shares in ORT to Abramovich.

That left TV-6 as Russia's last remaining independent television station. It quickly became the subject of a bankruptcy suit filed by

Lukoil-Garant, the pension fund of the Russian oil company Lukoil, which owned 15 percent of the station and was itself minority owned by the state. TV-6 argued that it was profitable by Western accounting standards. Nonetheless, the Supreme Arbitration Court ordered the station liquidated, and on January 14, 2002, the station was pulled off the air. With the actions against NTV, ORT, and TV-6, national television, the most important information source for 90 percent of the population, came entirely under the regime's control.

The takeover of television was accompanied by the subjugation of business. If under Yeltsin, corrupt businessmen and gangsters had privatized the state, under Putin, businessmen became serfs of the regime. The number of bureaucrats grew by nearly two-thirds, and this army of officials acted in their own predatory interests. In 1994, the Analytical Center for Social and Economic Policies of the Presidential Administration said that 70 to 90 percent of Russia's enterprises and banks in major cities were forced to pay criminal gangs 10 to 20 percent of their revenues.[13] The only thing that changed under Putin was the identity of those collecting the tribute. Now it went to government officials.[14]

The tax structure in Russia is such that if businesses paid all their taxes, they would not be profitable. As a result, businesses generally do not show their real revenues, a fact that is overlooked in exchange for bribes. Businessmen also pay bribes to get goods through customs, to acquire permits, to avoid fines after inspections, and just to be left alone. The system involves nearly everyone, which means that almost every citizen is vulnerable to facing criminal charges. The best way to avoid this fate is to show loyalty to the authorities.

In the early 2000s these practices faced only one serious challenge. It came from Mikhail Khodorkovsky, the head of the Yukos oil company and Russia's wealthiest man. His fate was a turning point in the consolidation of the system. Like other Yeltsin-era oligarchs, Khodorkovsky acquired his holdings through the corrupt privatization schemes, but he proved to be a very effective manager. He imported Western advisers and techniques and doubled the flow rate in his Western Siberian oil fields between 1997 and 2002.[15]

Khodorkovsky provoked a confrontation because, with the price of oil rising steadily, he realized that the best way to increase profits was to break with the Putin system and turn Yukos into a Western-style enterprise. He declared his income and introduced Western standards of accounting and corporate governance. He also competed with the government for influence in the State Duma, bribing deputies and supporting not only the liberal opposition parties, Yabloko and the Union of Right Forces, but also the communists.[16]

Putin normally controlled the Duma with the help of United Russia, the successor to the Unity Party, but as a result of Khodorkovsky's efforts, the government repeatedly failed in its attempts to increase taxes on the oil sector.[17] At the same time, Khodorkovsky began to accuse the government of corruption. The authorities' response was to arrest Khodorkovsky on October 25, 2003, and accuse him of fraud and tax evasion. The charges alleged that he avoided taxes by setting up intermediary firms in closed cities that offered tax advantages, and that he stole shares in a fertilizer plant during privatization. Similar charges could have been made against every Yeltsinera oligarch, but Khodorkovsky alone was prosecuted. He was sentenced to eight years in a labor camp, and Yukos was dismembered, with the pieces sold off cheaply to Putin's cronies. Near the end of his prison term, Khodorkovsky was charged again, this time with stealing the entire production of Yukos's subsidiaries, even though he had already been tried and sentenced for avoiding taxes on the sale of that production. In the second trial, he was sentenced to six and a half years.

After Khodorkovsky's arrest, there were no more attempts by Russian oligarchs to confront the Kremlin or finance the political opposition. On the contrary, the oligarchs, in their public statements and private gifts, tried to show total loyalty so as not to share Khodorkovsky's fate. With the Yukos case, the authorities made sure that private wealth could be used politically only in the service of the regime.

The arrest of Khodorkovsky and dismemberment of Yukos set a precedent that local officials were quick to follow. Property began to be seized all over the country through a process known as "raiding." In a Russian raid, an owner is typically charged with a crime by investigators in the pay of his economic competitors, who are often state officials or their close friends and relatives. The owner is then put in pretrial detention and given a below-market offer for his property. If this is not enough to persuade him to give up his business, a judge, in the pay of the raiders, can issue an order allowing the raiders to take it over.

An entire industry has grown up dedicated to taking companies away from their original owners. The cost of these operations was published in the Russian internet. It includes $50,000 to $200,000 for the relevant court decision, the most expensive and essential part; $10,000 to $60,000 to bribe the local police; and $100 to $200 per person to rent a group of thugs to move in and take over.[18] This system has put thousands of Russian businessmen into pretrial detention on criminal charges brought at the instigation of their competitors.[19]

Under the Putin regime's policies, the prime determinant of success in any venture was corrupt ties with the authorities. Officials at all levels waxed fat on a steady flow of bribes. Sergei Kanyev, a crime reporter for *Novaya Gazeta,* described the situation of a typical Moscow businessman. The businessman pays off all local officials. He gives the local police chief an expensive foreign car and treats his "curator" from the FSB to daily dinners in a restaurant. With the help of bribes, he maintains good relations with "the mayor, the tax inspectorate, the migration services, and the [public health authorities]. Once a month, the fire and trade inspectors visit his stores and they expect money or presents. The local beat officer comes by for a present on his birthday. In addition, the businessman makes payments to another pair of spongers, the head of the local branch of United Russia, and a representative from Just Russia," the other main pro-Kremlin party.

Street extortion, formerly the province of criminal gangs, is now carried out by the police. The warehouses are controlled by the commanders; shops and small restaurants by the criminal investigation unit; bootleggers and sellers of pirated DVDs by the anti–economic crimes unit. Vendors who sell in the markets are shaken down by the local beat officers, who also shake down illegal migrants and people who are drunk or caught urinating in public, guard spots where prostitutes gather, and shake down the prostitutes' clients.[20]

While private businesses were being bled by bureaucrats at every level, high-ranking officials were able to enrich themselves by stealing from the state after being put on the boards of state-run corporations. Dimitri Medvedev, when he was first deputy premier (before becoming president), was made the chairman of Gazprom. Igor Sechin, the deputy head of the Kremlin administration, became the chairman of the Rosneft oil company. Igor Shuvalov, an assistant to the president, was put on the board of Russian Railways. In 2007, the capitalization of Gazprom was $236 billion, Rosneft $94 billion, and Russian Railways $50 billion. Other state companies were similarly wealthy, and it was estimated that the people around Putin controlled companies that accounted for 80 percent of the capitalization of the Russian stock market.[21]

Access to the cash flows of huge state enterprises made it possible for Russian officials to channel business and stolen state resources to offshore companies that they secretly controlled. Putin's friend Leonid Reiman, the minister of telecommunications, was found by a Zurich arbitration tribunal in 2007 to have used his position as chairman of the board of the state-run telecommunications holding company to acquire assets valued at $6 billion.[22]

Putin himself is hardly uninvolved. Evidence suggests that he also pillages the state, on an even grander scale. Some of Russia's wealthiest men are Putin's personal friends, including Gennady Timchenko, the head of the Gunvor oil trading company, who is believed to be worth $15.3 billion; Yuri Kovalchuk, an owner of the Rossiya Bank ($1.4 billion); and the Rotenberg brothers, Arkady and Boris, whose combined wealth is estimated at $5.6 billion. All of these men made fortunes on the assets of the state. Gazfund, the largest nongovernment pension fund, Gazprombank, Russia's second–most important bank, and Gazprom-media were all removed from state-run Gazprom and put under the control of the Rossiya Bank. Gunvor, little known in 2000, has since become the world's third-largest oil trader, and the Rotenberg brothers, besides owning intermediary firms that sold pipes to Gazprom, received approximately $7 billion in contracts for the 2014 Sochi Olympics.[23]

According to Boris Nemtsov, the former first deputy prime minister who was murdered in Moscow on February 27, 2015, and Vladimir Milov, the former deputy minister of energy, "There is reason to assume that all of these Timchenkos, Kovalchuks, Rotenbergs—are nothing more than nominal owners of big property and that the real beneficiary is Putin himself."[24]

Stanislav Belkovsky, a Russian political analyst who once worked as a speechwriter for Berezovsky, told the German newspaper *Die Welt* in 2007 that Putin's secret assets were worth $40 billion, which would make him the richest man in Europe. Citing senior figures in the president's own administration as his sources, Belkovsky said that Putin was the beneficial owner of 75 percent of Gunvor, 37 percent of Surgutneftegaz (a principal supplier of oil for Gunvor), and 4.5 percent of Gazprom. This ownership structure was concealed behind a "nontransparent network of offshore companies," with the final points in Zug, Switzerland, and Lichtenstein. When asked whether he could prove his claims, Belkovsky said that Putin's wealth is no secret among the elites. "And you should note that Vladimir Vladimirovich [Putin] has never sued me."[25] Belkovsky's estimates of Putin's private wealth track closely with those of Western intelligence.

With national television and business under the regime's control, all that remained was to neutralize the parliament and the courts. This process, well advanced in the early years of Yeltsin's rule, reached its final expression under Putin. Under Yeltsin the State Duma was weak but not completely powerless, and there were possibilities for oppositionists to achieve representation. These possibilities were eliminated under Putin.

The dramatic rise in Russian living standards under Putin was of immense benefit to United Russia, which began actively recruiting new members and opening offices all over the country. The shift of power to the government bureaucracy and concentration of decision making in the hands of the president created a situation in which nearly everyone in a management position felt that he needed the protection of a good relationship with the authorities, which, as representatives of the regime made clear, was best guaranteed by donations and activism on behalf of United Russia.

One result of this changed situation was that the communists and the Liberal Democratic Party (LDPR), which had made at least a show of opposition during the Yeltsin period, all but surrendered their independence. They now supported the regime's policies while occasionally arguing about their implementation.

This left the members of the two liberal parties, Yabloko and the Union of Right Forces (SPS), as the only potential opposition voices in the Duma. After Khodorkovsky's arrest, however, both parties were starved of funds. At the same time, a law was passed raising the threshold for representation in the Duma to 7 percent, meaning that a party had to poll strongly all over the country to be represented. After 2007, neither Yabloko nor SPS was able to surmount this barrier, and their failure to gain places in the Duma all but eliminated liberals from the country's official political life. Parties not represented in the Duma could get on the ballot in future elections only by collecting tens of thousands of signatures, but another law permitted officials to reject a petition if even a single signature could not be verified. In 2007, People for Democracy and Justice, led by former prime minister Mikhail Kasyanov, was denied registration because of 37 mistakes in a list of more than 56,000 party members. In 2011, the Popular Freedom Party, the new party of Nemtsov and Kasyanov, was disqualified because of 79 irregularities in a list of 46,148 signatures.[26]

Since 2007, there have been only four parties in the Duma: United Russia, the Communists, LDPR, and Just Russia. In the 2012 presidential race, each of these parties fielded a candidate. A fifth candidate, Mikhail Prokhorov, collected enough signatures to be placed on the ballot and ran with the tacit approval of the authorities. Serious criticism of the regime or its policies played no role in the presidential race.

Despite the elimination of real political opposition, the regime tried to produce the highest possible vote totals for its candidates—members of United Russia in the parliamentary elections and Medvedev and Putin in the 2008 and 2012 presidential elections. Officials, managers, law enforcement officers, and businessmen were all expected to work for United Russia.

In twenty of the eighty-three Russian regions, including the North Caucasus, the South Urals, Tuva, and Kalmykia, there was virtually no local opposition and election returns were easily falsified. In the December 2011 parliamentary elections, for example, United Russia received more than 90 percent of the recorded vote in Dagestan and Ingushetiya and 99.48 percent in Chechnya.[27]

In other regions, where outright falsification met with more resistance, United Russia pressured voters to support its candidates "voluntarily." State employees were instructed to vote for the regime's candidates, and workers were frequently forced to vote at their place of work under the watchful eyes of their bosses, who were normally members of United Russia. In rural areas, people not supporting the authorities could have their water turned off or their houses burned down. The electoral results were reinforced by ballot-box stuffing, multiple voting, and the falsification of protocols.

Control over the electoral process was complemented by the subjugation of the judiciary, which had little ability to maintain its independence within an otherwise unitary government.

In every region, it is the court chairmen who organize the work of the court, including the assignment of cases. Before Putin, many chairmen fulfilled their responsibilities in a neutral manner, but in December 2001, chairmen began to be appointed by the president. This assured their subordination to the government.

The chairman is in direct contact with the political authorities and has many ways of controlling the judges in his or her district. He or she arranges housing for the judges and sets their vacation schedules. The chairman also collects material that can be used as grounds for a judge's dismissal—for example, that a judge is dilatory in hearing cases or commits procedural errors. He or she can also influence the qualification commission, a supervisory organ elected by the judges themselves, to make sure that a judge suspected of corruption is or is not investigated.[28]

Under these circumstances, judges are afraid to resist pressure from the court chairman. If a matter between individuals is before the court, it often is decided on its merits. But if there is "government interest" in a case, orders for its resolution are transmitted to the judge through the court chairman.[29]

The chairman of the Moscow City Court, Olga Yegorova, was particularly notorious for carrying out political orders and using her authority to punish judicial independence. In one famous instance, Judge Olga Kudeshkina was removed in May 2004 after stating publicly that Yegorova had ordered her to make a decision desired by the general prosecutor in the case of the Three Whales and Grand furniture chains, which were founded by the father of a high-ranking FSB official and had reportedly evaded millions of dollars in import duties.

The police investigator in the case was Pavel Zaitsev. After the case was closed on orders from the general prosecutor, the prosecutor's office brought charges against Zaitsev for conducting a search without authorization. Zaitsev said that he had to conduct an immediate search in order to prevent the destruction of records, a reason allowed under the law. The case was assigned to Kudeshkina, who was newly arrived in Moscow from Siberia.

Kudeshkina told journalists that before the trial started, Dmitri Shokhin, the prosecutor in the case, hinted to her that a guilty verdict was expected. The trial began in May 2003, and after a week, Shokhin began protesting against Kudeshkina's line of questioning, accusing her of favoring the accused. He turned to the lay jurors, members of the public who until 2004 served in Russian courts as monitors, and asked them to replace her. When they refused, he demanded that they be removed as well.[30]

Four days later, Kudeshkina was called in to see Yegorova, who, according to Kudeshkina's account, shouted at her and abused her. Yegorova phoned Yuri Biryukov, the deputy general prosecutor, and discussed the case in Kudeshkina's presence. She then faxed Biryukov copies of Shokhin's complaints. The same day, the lay jurors withdrew from the case. In written statements, they said that Shokhin's "disgusting" efforts to put pressure on them were damaging their health. Yegorova instructed Kudeshkina to exclude the jurors' statements from the case file and expunge them from the transcript. She refused, and Yegorova removed her from the case. Five months later, another judge found Zaitsev guilty and gave him a two-year suspended sentence.[31]

In November, Kudeshkina took a leave from the bench to run for the Duma. In her campaign she said that the courts were being used to settle "political, commercial and even personal scores."[32] She withdrew from the race days before the election after receiving threats, and the Moscow qualification commission began disciplinary proceedings against her for defaming the judiciary. In May 2004, the commission fired her from her judgeship, accusing her of seeking to denigrate the authority of the judges and undermine the prestige of the judicial profession.[33]

Kudeshkina's experience was emblematic. Russians do not expect and cannot obtain justice in any case where the regime's interests are involved, including the cases of those who exploit their political ties to amass wealth. The corruption of the judiciary in Russia is the reason the European Court is overwhelmed with complaints from Russia. In 2013, there were 24,102 complaints to the European Court from Russia, more than from any of the other forty-six countries that make up the Council of Europe. Most of these will never be heard, but of 129 judgments, all but 10 went against Russia.[34]

The situation was summed up by Alexander Konovalov, Russia's minister of justice, in an interview on NTV on June 2, 2008. "In developed countries," he said, "a person understands for what he can be seriously punished and where he is within his rights and can act calmly and with confidence and where he can turn for defense if his rights are violated.

"In our country, unfortunately . . . the ordinary person is deceived by everyone. . . . We have not overcome our hesitancy in the defense of our rights and their realization in general. . . . There was never was any respect for law in Russian life and there is none today."[35]

Putin and his underlings spoke of Russia "rising from its knees" after the chaos of the Yeltsin years. Behind the façade of rising wealth, however, Russia had come full circle. It had once again become a state that deprived its citizens of a voice or the means to defend their rights. The resulting system, however, is not prepared to withstand external political and economic shocks. It can be protected only through concealment or aggressive militarism if it is to stave off internal conflict and eventual collapse.

The Putin system divided Russian society into two groups, a handful who benefit from corruption and the vast majority who cannot. Such a division invites a violent crisis and, as a result of events in Ukraine, this is exactly what Russia got.

# 4

## Selective Terror

The Putin regime succeeded in creating the impression of stability. It was helped by the spirit of the times. Bureaucrats sucked money out of Russia at a phenomenal rate, but energy prices boomed and there were signs of the new prosperity everywhere. Dozens of coffeehouses appeared within the space of a few months. So did twenty-four-hour drugstores and shopping malls. Stores in Moscow sold the world's most expensive brands. Near the building that once housed the Military Colleagues of the Supreme Court, where thousands were sentenced to death during the Great Terror, there opened Bentley and Maserati dealerships and an Ermenegildo Zegna clothing store.

Deprived for decades of Western consumer goods, many Russians quickly became connoisseurs. Women in the capital spent 12 percent of their paychecks on cosmetics,[1] and the city's restaurants and cafés were crowded with the leisured and the fashionably dressed. Government officials bought apartments for their mistresses, helping to aggravate the housing shortage, and there was a boom in private planes and cosmetology. A sign of the times was a poster showing a beautiful woman telling her boyfriend, "With two kidneys, how can you say that you don't have enough money for gifts?"

The economic boom and a centralized system, however, could not by themselves ensure the regime's durability. The surface calm was also the product of provocation and terror. The terror served to remind everyone that behind the façade of a normal society, the regime had the ability to eliminate its enemies and, if threatened, would not hesitate to do so.

There was no mass repression. Most citizens had little to fear from the regime. Terror was focused instead on two goals: preventing any compromise over Chechnya and eliminating individuals who were thought to pose a serious threat to the emerging system.

For many Russians, defeat in the first Chechen war was a symbol of the country's humiliation under Yeltsin. The invasion of Chechnya in September 1999 made it possible to depict Putin as the person who was restoring the nation's honor and helped him win the presidency. To preserve Putin's image as a successful warrior, however, it was important that the Chechen resistance be destroyed.

The second Chechen war was pursued even more ruthlessly than the first. Russian aircraft bombed Chechnya indiscriminately. The Russians used ground-to-ground missiles and fuel air "vacuum" explosives, which have been compared to low-level tactical nuclear weapons, against populated areas. At the same time, thousands of Chechen males disappeared in security sweeps. The barbarity of Russian tactics prompted international pressure to end the war. But these efforts were defeated decisively with the help of two further provocations: the hostage siege at the Theater on Dubrovka in Moscow in October 2002 and the siege at a school in Beslan in September 2004.

The Dubrovka and Beslan hostage takings changed Russia in ways that were not fully appreciated at the time. Russia remained relatively free. But the KGB-FSB view of the supremacy of the state's interests and the negligible value of human life was affirmed and legitimized. In each case, a thousand or more hostages were seized by Chechen terrorists. In both instances, the Russian authorities refused to negotiate and acted instead to kill the terrorists as well as hundreds of hostages. And in both cases, there was evidence that the government had a role in instigating the original attacks.

The seizure of the Theater on Dubrovka took place during a performance of *Nord-Ost,* the most popular musical in Russia. On October 23, shortly after 9 PM, just as the audience was settling in for the second act, forty heavily armed male and female Chechen terrorists entered the theater and moved rapidly down the aisles in the semi-darkness. The men wore camouflage gear, had Kalashnikov assault rifles slung over their shoulders, and carried grenade launchers.

The terrorists moved large canvas bags into the middle of the stage and began taking out packets of explosives that the women attached to belts around their waists. The men meanwhile laid booby traps and taped explosive devices to the walls. They set up three large bombs—gas tanks with metal fragments inside and artillery shells as detonators: one in the middle of the first floor, another in the middle of the balcony, and a third in the center of the stage. The bombs were placed so that if they went off at once, the entire audience would be caught in a hail of shrapnel and the force would cause the building to collapse.

The ostensible leader of the terrorists was Movsar Baraev, nephew of the Chechen kidnapper Arbi Baraev, who, according to the military newspaper *Krasnaya Zvezda,* participated in the murder of 170 people. There were signs, however, that the person actually in charge was another terrorist, "Abubakar" (Ruslan Elmurzaev). The terrorists demanded an immediate end to the war in Chechnya. They warned that if any one of them were killed, they would kill ten hostages in response. "We've come to . . . stop the war or to die for Allah," Baraev said. "We desire death more than you desire life."[2]

The hostages were allowed to use their cell phones. They told relatives to beg the authorities to negotiate with the terrorists and not to attack the theater. In the early hours of the siege, the terrorists released more than a hundred hostages: children under twelve, Muslims, foreigners, and people with serious medical conditions. A series of intermediaries, including the politicians Grigory Yavlinsky, Irina Khakamada, and Ruslan Aushev, and the journalist Anna Politkovskaya, attempted to negotiate with the terrorists, but at first the terrorists had trouble formulating their demands. They finally said that if Putin announced an end to the war and pulled troops out of one Chechen region within twenty-four hours, the hostages would go free. The Russian response was to offer the terrorists safe passage if they left the building, which, under the circumstances, resembled a nonoffer.

For forty-eight hours, the hostages lived in a state of extreme tension, whiplashed between dull apprehension and crippling fear, unable to leave their seats except to relieve themselves in the orchestra pit, which became a public toilet, and too agitated to sleep. But on the evening of October 25, the authorities suddenly agreed to negotiate. They announced that Victor Kazantsev, Putin's envoy in the Southern Federal District, would arrive at the theater at 10 the next morning to begin talks. The news changed the atmosphere in the theater. Baraev got up on the stage and said, "Everything is going according to plan. We do not want to kill you."[3] Some of the terrorists gathered in a sound booth to watch a videotape of their takeover of the theater. The hostages started exchanging email addresses and phone numbers. A few of the women took out mirrors and began combing their hair. Most of them, overcome by fatigue, fell into a deep sleep.[4]

At 5 AM, the FSB forces began pumping lethal gas into the theater through the ventilation system. After waiting about fifteen minutes for the gas to take effect, members of the FSB's Alfa and Wympel units equipped with flak jackets, gas masks, and assault weapons entered the building in a two-pronged assault from the front and rear and began executing the terrorists. The first group killed a large number of terrorists who had been forced backward onto the stage. The other group ran up the stairs and along the corridors to the storeroom that had served as the terrorists' headquarters, killing as they went, encountering ineffectual resistance. Many of the terrorists, including almost all of the female suicide bombers, were overcome by the gas. They were executed while unconscious.

In a few minutes, all forty terrorists had been killed. They had had time to realize that the hall was being filled with gas but did not open fire on the hostages or kill them with grenades. None of the explosives with which they had threatened to blow up the building were detonated. It was later discovered that the bombs were dummies, as were many of the women's suicide belts. All of the members of the Alfa and Wimpel units survived the storm. But in the theater, more than eight hundred unconscious hostages were slumped in their seats or lying in the aisles, finding it difficult to breathe.

The evacuation of the hostages took place amid chaos. In the absence of medical personnel, police and soldiers draped the bodies of comatose hostages over their shoulders or carried them out by the arms and legs. Bodies were piled one on top of another outside the theater entrance, with no attempt to separate the living from the dead. Although the medical authorities had had days to prepare for the aftermath of the siege, there was a shortage of ambulances, and hostages were taken to hospitals in buses, microbuses, and cars.[5] Many died as a result. Alexander Karpov, a well-known songwriter, died after spending seven hours alive in a bus packed with corpses.[6]

In another case, thirty hostages were put in a twelve-seat military microbus, some on the floor. A thirteen-year-old girl was crushed under the bodies and died on the way to a hospital.[7]

The gas was not identified for the rescuers, who were forced to spend several hours testing antidotes before they found one that was effective—naloxone, which is used to treat heroin overdoses.[8] The discovery came too late to save many lives. The confusion continued at the hospitals, where hundreds of hostages suffering exposure to an unknown gas suddenly appeared, overwhelming the hospital's ability to treat them. The FSB, apparently aware that the death toll was going to be shocking, initially deliberately understated the fatalities. The first report was that 10 people had died, leading Russians to feel a sense of relief. In the next twenty-four hours, the number of deaths was revised steadily upward from 10 to 30 to 67 to 90 to 100 to 118. The final official death count for the hostages from the gas was 129.[9]

The storming of the theater significantly boosted Putin's popularity. He depicted the operation as a decisive Russian victory over terror. But in the weeks following the storm, there began to be serious doubts about the regime's actions and fears that, once again, the entire episode might have been a provocation. On November 6, eleven days after the attack, the Kovalev commission, which was investigating the apartment bombings, added the Dubrovka siege as a subject of inquiry.[10] One of the siege's most puzzling aspects was that with a war going on and the police and the public on heightened alert, a small army of terrorists was able to assemble in Moscow and spend months preparing a coordinated attack without being detected.

Preparations for the attack had begun in April 2002, when a terrorist linked to Shamil Basaev bought a house in the village of Chernoe, in the Moscow oblast, and began to receive visitors and a stream of weapons from the North Caucasus. Neither the police nor the FSB reacted to this highly unusual activity. The FSB also did not react to warnings from sources in the criminal world that a large group of armed Chechen extremists had gathered in the central and southwest districts of Moscow. One warning came from Mikhail Trepashkin, who was no longer in the FSB but had stayed in touch with his criminal contacts. He informed the FSB, among other things, that Abubakar had been living in Moscow and was running protection for two firms that were providing money to the Chechen rebels. After the attack, when Trepashkin learned of Abubakar's role, he again contacted the FSB and offered to share information. They reacted by trying to fabricate a case against him.[11]

The security services may have done more than fail to stop the preparations. There were signs that the FSB and the terrorists were closely connected. One of the visitors to the house in Chernoe was Arman Menkeev, a retired major in Russian military intelligence (GRU) and a specialist in the making of explosives. He reportedly prepared the suicide bombers' explosives belts and other devices used by the hostage takers. Menkeev did not take part in the actual hostage taking, but his role is hard to understand if the authorities were not facilitating the attack. FSB officers interrogating Menkeev after the siege concluded that he was loyal to the Russian government and, moreover, "knows how to keep a military secret."[12]

Other terrorists had recently been in Russian custody. Movsar Baraev was jailed in August after being arrested by the GRU, but was released in time to play a leading role in the hostage taking.[13] At least three of the female suicide bombers in the theater were in custody in September, a month before the attack, but they too were freed in time to participate. A fourth was supposedly serving a long sentence in a Russian labor camp. Her mother recognized her on television during the siege and, according to Novaya Gazeta, did not understand how her daughter had gotten to Moscow from her prison cell.[14]

Eight of the female suicide bombers, according to Alexander Khinshtein, an investigative journalist, were able to take up residence in former military housing on Ilovaiskaya Street, not far from the theater, where illegal residents paid bribes and were apparently under the protection of members of the Moscow police.[15]

It also struck many as strange that with the public transfixed by the horror of nearly a thousand people taken hostage, the authorities immediately used the crisis for political advantage. The hostage takers identified themselves as Islamists, but the authorities blamed the attack on Aslan Maskhadov, Chechnya's president and the leader of the non-Islamist separatists. This suggested that the authorities actually wanted a bloody denouement. In a confrontation between Islamists and the government, Maskhadov, as Chechnya's last elected leader, was probably the only person capable of negotiating a peaceful resolution.

When the terrorists seized the theater, Ahmed Zakaev, Maskhadov's overseas representative, said that Maskhadov, who was in hiding in the mountains of Chechnya, condemned the attack and called for a peaceful end to the crisis. The Russian media, however, said that the attack was ordered by Maskhadov. The web site Newsru .com cited a tape shown on Al Jazeera Television in which Maskhadov said, "In the very near future, we will conduct an operation which will overturn the history of the Chechen war." The FSB said that this was proof that Maskhadov was behind the *Nord-Ost* attack, and a Putin spokesman said that the Chechen president had to be "wiped out."[16]

The tape shown on Russian television, however, was only a fragment of the original. From the original it was clear that the tape was made not on the eve of the theater siege but at least two months earlier, at the end of the summer. This supported Zakaev's statement that Maskhadov was referring not to the seizure of hostages but to an impending military operation against federal forces. When the terrorists were asked in an interview on NTV who had sent them, Baraev said that they had been sent by Maskhadov's Islamist rival, Shamil Basaev.[17]

In the months after the *Nord-Ost* attack, family members and survivors began to demand answers from the authorities. The first question concerned the identity of the gas. The authorities would say only that the gas had been a calmative opiate, a derivative of fenatyl delivered in aerosol form. The precise chemical was never identified. According to some sources, the agent was Kolokol-1, an incapacitating gas developed in a Soviet military laboratory in the 1970s that carries a high risk of death.[18]

This question was not trivial. Many of the survivors were seriously ill, and without knowing the identity of the poison, doctors did not know how to treat them. In April 2003, a lawyer representing some of the former hostages said that approximately forty more had died since October 26, 2002. In October 2003, the newspaper *Versiya,* summing up the results of its own investigation, said that about three hundred of the former hostages were now dead.[19]

On September 30, 2003, in answer to questions from journalists, Putin said that the gas was "harmless" and denied that it caused the hostages' deaths. They had died from long periods of immobility, he said, and from chronic diseases. But experts from the Center for Catastrophic Medicine concluded that the deaths were caused by exposure to a "high concentration of a chemical substance."[20]

One of the surviving hostages who became concerned about the possible ties between the terrorists and the authorities was Vesselin

Nedkov, a Bulgarian who, on the first night of the siege, noticed that a man appeared in the theater wearing a suit instead of camouflage gear. He was cheered by the terrorists. "Was everything normal?" one of the Chechens asked the new arrival in Russian. "Of course," he replied. "Fifty rubles here, fifty rubles there. I came in the normal way."[21] Nedkov was already shocked that a large group of terrorists carrying bombs and grenade launchers could take over a theater in the center of Moscow, but the ability of one of the terrorists to enter the building even after it was surrounded by police astonished him even more. Were the authorities the solution, he asked himself, or part of the problem?

I was in Moscow at the time of the *Nord-Ost* siege, and like nearly everyone in the city, I prayed for the hostages' safety. I went to the scene but, like other journalists, could get no closer than the police lines. What I was able to reconstruct about the events in the months after the storm, however, convinced me that the authorities facilitated the takeover of the theater.

All of the terrorists were executed, including many who were shot while unconscious. This made no sense if the Russian authorities hoped to learn about the organization of the attack and any plans for future attacks. It was logical, however, if the authorities wanted to make sure that there could be no public trial at which inconvenient details could be revealed.

At the same time, relatives of victims and survivors who filed suit against the Moscow city government in an attempt to learn more about what had happened faced bureaucratic harassment from the authorities. A request by human rights groups to the prosecutor to open an investigation into the use of the gas was denied. A motion to open a parliamentary inquiry into the siege was voted down. Sergei Yushchenkov, the head of a commission investigating the apartment bombings, promised to investigate the *Nord-Ost* attack as well but was assassinated on April 17, 2003. At a press conference on the third anniversary of the events, Svetlana Gubareva, who lost her American fiancé, Sandy Booker, and her thirteen-year-old daughter Sasha in the siege, said, "The impression is created that all of us—former hostages living and dead and relatives of hostages—for the [authorities] are absolutely nobody."[22]

Before the seizure of the theater, the Russian authorities were under mounting pressure to reach a settlement over Chechnya. The Russian population was growing tired of the war, which had been going on for three years. In a September 2002 poll, 56 percent of respondents favored peace negotiations to end the Chechen conflict, while only 34 percent supported continued military action.[23] There was also growing international pressure for a settlement. On August 16–19, 2002, talks took place between former speakers of the Russian parliament, Ivan Rybkin and Ruslan Khasbulatov, and Chechen leader Akhmed Zakaev under the auspices of the American Committee for Peace in Chechnya, one of whose leading figures was Zbigniew Brzezinski. Under a plan proposed by Brzezinski, Chechens would acknowledge Russian territorial integrity and a referendum would be held under which the Chechens could approve the constitutional basis of extensive self-government. The theater siege, however, brought these talks to an end.

With pressure for a settlement removed, the regime was free to carry out its preferred strategy, in which a pro-Moscow puppet government headed by the former rebel Ramzan Kadyrov was given nearly complete freedom to act inside Chechnya as long as it professed loyalty to Moscow. Russia also gave billions of rubles in aid.

Much of this money was stolen, but some was used in reconstruction. The security organs were staffed by ethnic Chechens, who were as cruel as their Russian predecessors but more selective. Rebels were offered amnesty and the possibility to return home. Abducted people no longer inevitably disappeared. These tactics and exhaustion after nearly a decade of war split the ranks of the resistance, and the fighting declined.

Reduced violence in Chechnya, however, came alongside an increase in fighting in the neighboring republics, particularly Ingushetiya. Murat Zyazikov, an FSB veteran who was elected president of Ingushetiya in a rigged election, responded to attacks with hundreds of summary executions, which led to a massive influx of young men into the insurgents' ranks.[24] On June 21, 2004, Chechen and Ingush militants led by Basaev carried out a large-scale attack on government buildings in Nazran, the Ingush capital, including the Interior Ministry. The Russians were taken completely by surprise, and scores of police and security personnel were killed.

By the summer of 2004, both the Chechen resistance and the Russian authorities were considering ways to reassert their positions. The radical Islamist wing of the resistance knew that it would take something spectacular to force the Russians to negotiate over Chechnya, and resistance leaders wanted to show that the war was continuing. The Russians wanted to deliver a decisive blow to the resistance and confirm the success of their policies. This situation led to the spawning of plots on both sides. The result was the seizure by Chechen terrorists of a school in the city of Beslan in North Ossetia on September 1, 2004.

The morning of September 1 in Beslan was sunny and warm. Children in blue and white school uniforms arrived at School No. 1

with their parents for the Ceremony of the First Bell. Music was playing over the loudspeakers and many of the children were carrying balloons. By 9 AM, there were more than a thousand people in the schoolyard.

Just as the formalities were about to begin, scores of terrorists in military clothes invaded the schoolyard, firing machine guns in the air. Many parents did not spot the terrorists at first and did not realize the significance of the shots. But the firing continued, with the terrorists shouting, "Allahu Akbar" and "Get into the school" and herding the parents, teachers, and children first into the school and then into the gymnasium, which was twenty-five yards long by ten yards wide.

With each flood of arrivals, the noise and panic increased. Finally, a male hostage approached one of the terrorists and was immediately shot in the head. Other male hostages were forced to drag his corpse by the arms through the gym, and the crowd suddenly became quiet. The terrorists hung bombs packed with ball bearings and shards of glass from a wire strung across the gym and pulled up floorboards to put bombs beneath. They put the largest devices on chairs in the midst of the hostages.

The terrorists, almost all Chechens or Ingush, were led by Ruslan Khuchbarov, known as "the Colonel." In 1998 he had murdered two Armenian men in a dispute over a woman, and in the aftermath he became "deeply religious." Khuchbarov's second in command was Vladimir Khodov, a half-Ukrainian, half-Ossetian convert to Islam who had committed rapes in 1998 and 2004 and was involved in a car bombing in Vladikavkaz in March and a train derailment in Elkhotovo two months later.[25]

After the terrorists established control, they sent out a note with Larissa Mamitova, one of the hostages, in which they demanded that four people come to the school: Alexander Dzasokhov, the president of North Ossetia; Ingush President Zyazikov; Aslambek Aslakhanov, an adviser to Putin on the North Caucasus; and Leonid Roshal, a pediatrician who was believed to have worked with the FSB during the *Nord-Ost* siege. The note also contained a cell phone number for contacting the terrorists. A second hostage was sent out with a video of the situation inside the school as well as a second note demanding a halt to the war in Chechnya and the release of twenty-seven rebels captured after the June raid in Ingushetiya.

Despite the notes, however, the authorities showed no interest in negotiating. State television reported that the hostages were making no demands, and although Mamitova insisted to the authorities that more than a thousand were held captive in the school, state television gave the number as 120.[26]

The lies enraged the terrorists. They told the hostages that their lives had already been written off and forbade them to drink water or go to the toilet. They then separated out the younger men and led them to a small room, where they were forced to sit facing the wall with their arms over their heads. The male terrorists then withdrew, and the female terrorists in the room detonated their bomb belts, causing an enormous explosion, killing most of the men instantly. Others suffered horrible injuries. One man lost his legs and buttocks but was still alive. The male terrorists returned after the explosion and forced the few survivors to carry the dead and injured to a room on an upper floor, where the injured were reportedly beaten to death. The dead were then thrown out of the window.[27] According to a report on the siege by a North Ossetian parliamentary commission, the murder of the young adult male hostages was a direct response to the authorities' refusal to acknowledge the terrorists' demands.[28]

At 11:30 AM, Dzasokhov arrived in Beslan and organized a crisis committee that also included Teimuraz Mamsurov, the chairman of the North Ossetian parliament. But Dzasokhov was soon forced to hand over authority to Vasily Andreev, the head of the North Ossetian FSB. Two deputy directors of the FSB, Vladimir Pronichev and Vladimir Anisimov, arrived from Moscow and set up a parallel operational headquarters that had very little contact with the crisis committee. From that point, all of the real decisions were taken by the FSB.

Dzasokhov announced that he was ready to enter the school, but he was warned by the operational headquarters that he would be stopped if he tried.[29] The cell phone number that the terrorists had sent out with Mamitova was mysteriously blocked, and the video cassette sent out with the second hostage was declared "empty" (the video was shown several days later on NTV).[30] When the terrorists saw that the cell phone number was not working, they sent Mamitova out of the school a second time with a new number. At that point, Vitaly Zangionov, a negotiator from the North Ossetian FSB, was appointed to talk to the terrorists, but his offers—an escape route, money, and a human shield—were irrelevant to the terrorists' demands. If the authorities had agreed at least to free the twenty-seven imprisoned terrorists who took part in the raid on Ingushetiya, they might have bought the lives of many hostages. This strategy was not attempted.

In the meantime, the FSB was almost certainly responsible for eliminating one more potential negotiator, Anna Politkovskaya. After hearing about the hostage taking, Politkovskaya boarded a 9 PM flight for Rostov, hoping to proceed to Beslan by car. She was respected by Chechens for her reporting and had more success in the *Nord-Ost* crisis than other negotiators. After boarding the plane for

Rostov, however, she took a sip of tea and lost consciousness. When the plane landed, she was rushed to a hospital and put in intensive care. She was later told that she had been poisoned.

On the second day of the siege, state-run television announced that it had the exact number of hostages in the school—354. The real figure was 1,128. The terrorists who had access to radio and television and the hostages who were close enough to hear were stunned as reporters repeatedly gave out this absurdly understated estimate.[31]

As the siege wore on, the condition of the hostages deteriorated. They were packed inside the gymnasium with barely enough room to move. It was a hot day and the heat in the gym became unbearable, making it difficult to breathe. Many of the hostages, prevented from drinking, were dehydrated and beginning to slip in and out of consciousness. The terrorists brought in buckets for the hostages to relieve themselves into. The smell of waste soon became overpowering. At the same time, ravaged by thirst, the hostages began to drink their own urine.

Despite the worsening humanitarian crisis, the authorities did not speak to the terrorists. Instead, tanks and armored personnel carriers were brought up to Beslan from Vladikavkaz. The only real negotiation was with Ruslan Aushev, the former president of Ingushetiya, on September 2. Aushev called the terrorists on his own initiative, and they agreed to let him enter the school. He was led inside at 3:30 PM by masked terrorists and brought to see the Colonel, who told him the terrorists were acting on the orders of Shamil Basaev. Aushev was able to secure the release of eleven women and fifteen nursing infants and toddlers.[32] He was also given a note to Putin from Basaev, in which Basaev described himself as a "slave of Allah" and called for independence for Chechnya in exchange for security for Russia. If Chechnya were given independence, Basaev wrote, it would not conclude any military or political agreements directed against Russia, would join the Commonwealth of Independent States, and would remain in the ruble zone. Finally, he said that the Chechen rebels had no part in the 1999 apartment building bombings but were willing to take responsibility for them "under certain circumstances."[33] This appeared to be an offer—from one terrorist to another—to help conceal the real authors of the bombings.

Several times on September 2, Russian officials gave interviews in which they said they had no intention of storming the school. At 2 PM, in his first public comments on the attack, Putin said that the chief task was saving the lives of the hostages and that everything would be subordinated to that goal. Andreev, the head of the crisis committee, announced that there could be no question of using force in this situation and that the authorities faced a period of "long and intensive negotiations."[34]

Meanwhile, Russian Special Forces were secretly rehearsing a storm of the school, taking over an abandoned school in the village of Farn, less than a mile outside Beslan. The sight of armed men seizing the school created panic among village residents, who thought the building was being taken over by terrorists. When the local police went to investigate, they found that the terrorists were Special Forces. Word of the exercise spread to Beslan, where the relatives of the hostages became convinced that, regardless of their public statements, the authorities fully intended to storm the school. From September 1 on, parents of the hostages gathered in front of the school and formed a human chain to prevent an attack. They were constantly told to leave but many refused.

While Aushev was arranging to enter the school, he and Dzasokhov were also on the phone to Zakaev in London; they asked him to contact Maskhadov. Zakaev could not call Maskhadov directly. For security reasons, he had to wait for Maskhadov to call. But Zakaev called the Chechen Service of Radio Liberty and told them of his talks with Aushev and Dzasokhov. Radio Liberty broadcast the news and, at his secret headquarters in the mountains, Maskhadov heard the broadcast and immediately called Zakaev. When Zakaev explained the situation, Maskhadov said he was ready to come to Beslan without preconditions if he was given safe passage.[35] He issued a statement calling on the terrorists to free the children.

During the second night of the siege, the hostages were becoming increasingly desperate and depressed. Some were hysterical. Others, particularly among the youngest children, were suffering from paralysis and were in danger of losing consciousness.

On the morning of September 3, Aushev and Dzasokhov again called Zakaev, who told them of Maskhadov's reaction. Dzasokhov said, "I did not expect anything else from Aslan Alievich." Dzasokhov said he needed two hours to resolve the question of safe passage, which he would have to discuss with "the first" (Putin).[36] A short time later, however, a person from FSB headquarters came to the crisis committee and told Dzasokhov that the operational staff knew about his contacts with Zakaev and Maskhadov, and the relatives of the hostages wanted to talk to him.

Dzasokhov emerged from his headquarters and went to a nearby club where many of the relatives were waiting for him. After being told that Dzasokhov had spoken to Maskhadov, they had left their posts in front of the school, where they were prepared to use their bodies to prevent Russian forces from storming the school. Dzasokhov said the situation was grim but that Maskhadov's intervention gave cause for hope. He said steps were being taken to assure Maskhadov's safe arrival in Beslan. Troops began their assault on the school minutes later.

The attack started with two explosions. According to Yuri Saveliev, a member of the parliamentary commission appointed to investigate the massacre, the first explosion was the result of the impact of a thermobaric grenade that was shot by either a flamethrower or a grenade launcher from a five-story building at 37 School Lane at 1:03 PM. The second explosion, twenty-two seconds later, was caused by a splinter grenade with an explosive power of thirteen pounds of TNT, fired by a grenade launcher from the five-story building at 41 School Lane.[37]

The first explosion started a fire in the school's attic. The second blew a hole in the wall of the gymnasium. These explosions, which state television attributed to the terrorists, were the signal to begin a storm of the school by Russian Special Forces. In the confusion, some hostages managed to escape. Others were taken by the terrorists to the cafeteria, assembly hall, and southern wing. But hundreds were trapped in the gymnasium, where the ceiling rafters were burning and beginning to fall on them. At 1:30, the Russian forces began to bombard the school with tanks, grenade launchers, and flamethrowers. The burning roof burst into flames and collapsed onto the hostages.

In the cafeteria, the terrorists placed women and children in the window openings, but Russian forces fired at the windows, killing them. They then, according to hostage accounts, began sweeping the cafeteria area with automatic-weapons fire.

Three mushroom-like clouds rose over the school, two white and one black. A videotape showed that at 3:08 PM, the school was still under massive fire from grenade launchers and flamethrowers. Tanks belonging to the 58th Army were also firing at the school. In all, the tape showed thirteen explosions. It was only at 3:10 PM that the head of the Special Forces, General Alexander Tikhonov, gave an order to begin putting out the fire. Until that time, for more than two hours, Tikhonov had *forbidden* anyone from extinguishing it. By the time the fire began to be suppressed at 3:28 PM, more than 160 hostages had been burned alive. The autopsies listed thermal shock as the cause of death, meaning that almost 100 percent of the victims' skin had been scorched. The hostages showed no wounds from bullets or fragments.[38]

When the firing ceased, 318 hostages were dead, including 186 children. Ten soldiers from the Russian Special Forces were also killed by the terrorists, as were two rescuers.[39] Thirty-two terrorists were killed, while an unknown number managed to escape.[40]

Putin arrived in Beslan at 5 AM. He went directly to the district hospital and spent thirty minutes visiting victims in their rooms. He then went to the FSB operational headquarters, where he met with officials and made a televised statement. There had been no intention to use force, he said, but events had moved "quickly and unexpectedly," and he praised the special services for their "particular courage." He then returned to Moscow without meeting with relatives of the victims or, apparently, visiting the burned school.[41] Later, Putin went on television to address the nation. "A terrible tragedy has taken place," he said. "We live in the conditions formed after the collapse of an enormous great state [the USSR]. . . . We exhibited weakness, and the weak are beaten."[42] He announced a set of measures supposedly designed to strengthen the country's unity. One was the abolition of the popular election of governors, a direct violation of the Russian Constitution.

While it was going on, the Beslan school crisis riveted the world's attention. Once it ended, further developments were largely ignored.

On September 4, 2004, the day after the attack by the Special Forces, the debris from the school, including children's notebooks and the body parts of the victims, was scooped up by an excavator, loaded onto trucks, and taken to a garbage dump outside of town. This destruction of evidence made it impossible to establish fully the sequence of events.

The survivors, however, wanted justice, and they were plunged into emotional turmoil as they listened to the version of events put forward by the Russian authorities, who blamed the terrorists, exonerated officials of any wrongdoing (many of them were later promoted), and refused to listen to the survivors' accounts of what they had seen and experienced.

In their despair, some of the parents turned to a cult leader to help resurrect their dead children. Others began their own investigation. They were joined by two journalists, Marina Litvinovich, editor of the site Pravdabeslana.ru, and Elena Milashina, a reporter for *Novaya Gazeta*. The North Ossetian parliament organized an investigative commission, and Yuri Saveliev, despite being a member of the commission, also began his own, independent investigation.

Although the authorities put sole blame for the attack on the Chechen terrorists, and Putin, in the aftermath of the tragedy, suggested that the terrorists enjoyed the support of the West, the evidence showed that the Beslan terrorist attack, like the *Nord-Ost* hostage siege, was also the result of a Russian provocation.

In August 2004, according to police documents obtained by *Novaya Gazeta*, warnings to the authorities about an impending terrorist attack in North Ossetia began arriving with chilling regularity. The last one came on September 1. At 5 AM, the Russian internal affairs ministry was informed by the Chechen police that a man named

Arsamikov, whom they had under arrest, said that there were plans by terrorists on that day to seize a school in Beslan. This gave the authorities four hours to avert the seizure. Not only was no action taken, but all roadblocks on the route to the school were mysteriously removed, giving the terrorists unhindered access.[43]

Of the eighteen terrorists who were later positively identified, the majority were supposed to have been in prison. Khodov, the subject of a federal search after his participation in the two terrorist attacks in 2004 in Vladikavkaz and Elkhotovo, nonetheless lived openly in Elkhotovo through the spring and summer, praying daily in the local mosque. His presence was reported to the North Ossetia FSB and the police organized crime division, but he was not arrested.[44]

The official investigation into Beslan did not address the question of why the police did not react to warnings and why known terrorists were allowed to roam free. But an explanation came from the author of the Beslan tragedy, Shamil Basaev. In a letter entitled "We have a lot to tell about Beslan . . . ," published on August 31, 2005, on the separatist web site Kavkazcenter.net, Basaev wrote that the seizure of the school began with a plan by the Russian security services to provoke Chechen rebels into trying to seize the North Ossetian Parliament and government buildings.

According to Basaev, the terrorist acts Khodov committed in 2004 were carried out with the help of the FSB to win Basaev's trust. Once he had done so, Khodov proposed a plan for seizing the North Ossetian government buildings. But after he confessed to Basaev that he was working for the FSB, Basaev persuaded him to become a double agent. In that capacity, he led the Russians to believe the plot was operational and scheduled for September 6, the anniversary of Chechen independence. The FSB, Basaev wrote, "intended [on

September 6] to meet the group as they entered Vladikavkaz and destroy them. On August 31, they opened a corridor for us for the active collection of intelligence but we used it to enter Beslan [and seize the school], changing the date and objective of the attack."[45]

Basaev cannot be treated as completely reliable, but his account is the only logical explanation of why the attack was not prevented. Moreover, the Maskhadov-led non-Islamic opposition conducted its own investigation and concluded that Basaev's explanation was accurate. The foiled takeover of government buildings in North Ossetia was meant to justify the abolition of the direct election of governors, a measure that had long been planned in order to reinforce Putin's hold on power.

There was no greater outrage over the authorities' role in the Beslan crisis than in Beslan itself. Relatives of the victims organized themselves into a group called "Mothers of Beslan" (later "Voice of Beslan") to investigate why the authorities had attacked a gymnasium packed with helpless hostages after agreement had been reached on negotiations that might have ended the crisis without further loss of life. The authorities insisted that it was necessary for the Special Forces to storm the building after the terrorists set off bombs. But survivors of the siege said there was no explosion inside the school, and that the storming began after the school was attacked with flamethrowers and grenade launchers from the outside. When officials denied that the Russian forces used flamethrowers, the relatives recovered used tubes from flamethrowers near the school and presented them to reporters.

In May 2005, the relatives of the victims wrote to Putin, saying they had detailed information about the crisis and were ready to come to Moscow, on foot if necessary, to present it. They received no reply.[46] On August 1, they issued a statement that they still wanted to meet Putin in Moscow, but that he was not welcome in Beslan on the September 1 anniversary of the attack. In response, Putin proposed a meeting with the relatives on September 2, in the middle of the ceremonies marking the tragedy.[47]

The offer split the relatives; some thought it should be ignored. In the end, however, three mothers left the ceremonies and went to Moscow, where they met with Putin for three hours. He said the meeting had been delayed to allow time to gather information.[48] But when the mothers asked how the terrorists were able to travel to Beslan undetected, why there was no attempt to negotiate, and why the crime scene was destroyed, Putin said he had no information. He promised a thorough investigation.[49] The investigation, whose results were announced in December, absolved the police and other security forces of any blame for the tragedy.

The seizure of the school by Chechen Islamist rebels firmly identified all Chechens with terrorists. But the bloody denouement of the crisis was also the responsibility of the Russian authorities, who gave no thought to the lives of hundreds of hostages who had become prisoners as a direct result of the authorities' incompetence and adventurism.

Although his intervention had represented the only hope of avoiding a massacre, the Russians blamed Maskhadov for the school seizure and announced that there was a bounty on his head. On March 8, 2005, Maskhadov was killed in a shoot-out in the Chechen town of Tolstoy-Yurt. In keeping with a Russian law that the bodies of "terrorists" are not returned to their families, his remains were disposed of secretly.[50]

In the months after the Beslan incident, questions were raised in Russia about the possible complicity of the Russian secret services, but ten years of conflict had blunted the public sense of right and wrong regarding Chechnya. Except among a few individuals in Moscow and the relatives of the victims in Beslan, interest in what actually had happened all but disappeared.

The *Nord-Ost* and Beslan hostage takings were immensely helpful to Putin's efforts to depict himself as a foe of terrorism and to legitimize the war in Chechnya to both Russia and the West. In Chechnya itself, Kadyrov ruled with the help of torture and disappearances, but Chechnya had faded from the world's consciousness. The notion that Putin was restoring order there became widely accepted.

In addition to destroying the separatist movement in Chechnya, Putin's regime consolidated its control by another method: the murders of well-known political figures. Russians could speak freely, and there was wide discussion in the independent press. The average citizen did not fear death at the hands of the authorities for political reasons. But selective killings made it clear that opposition in Russia was tolerated only within certain limits. If someone crossed an invisible line, which was subject to change, he did so at the risk of his life.

Two types of people who were vulnerable to assassination were the regime's opponents and its inconvenient friends. When opponents were murdered, the motive was usually deducible. When the victims were friends who had become a problem, the reasons were often more difficult to surmise.

Perhaps the best-known killing of a political opponent was that of Alexander Litvinenko, a fugitive FSB agent who wrote books about the apartment bombings and the FSB's links to organized crime. Litvinenko also contributed articles to Chechen rebel sites in which he ridiculed the FSB and Putin personally. His murder, November 23, 2006, was the world's first clear case of nuclear poisoning, and there were diverse theories about the motive. Many assumed he was killed because of his writings. It is more likely, however, that the problem was not what he wrote but who he was. FSB agents are expected to be totally dedicated to the regime. There must never arise a situation in which they go into opposition. Litvinenko, by his example, showed that even FSB agents could think and act on their own. In an FSB-dominated regime, this was a challenge that could not be ignored.

Litvinenko became ill on November 1 after drinking tea with Andrei Lugovoi, the owner of a Moscow security company, and Lugovoi's associate, Dmitri Kovtun, in the Pine Bar of the Millennium Hotel in London. For the next two days he suffered from vomiting and diarrhea. His hair began falling out, and there was a sharp drop in his white blood cell count. Litvinenko's doctors suspected radiation poisoning, but only gamma and beta particles can penetrate the skin, and there was no gamma or beta radiation in his blood. On November 20, he was moved to intensive care, where a photographer slipped into the ward and took a picture of him, wasted and bald, staring at the camera. This photo was featured on front pages all over the world.[51] On November 22 his condition worsened and his heart stopped twice. The next evening he was pronounced dead.

Litvinenko's friend Alexander Goldfarb read a statement from Litvinenko in which he accused Putin of his murder. "You may succeed in silencing one man," the statement said, "but the howl of protest from around the world will reverberate, Mr. Putin, in your ears for the rest of your life."[52]

Litvinenko died without knowing exactly what killed him, but on the eve of his death, samples of his urine were sent to the Atomic Weapons Establishment (AWE), which monitors Britain's nuclear weapons arsenal. There it was tested for alpha-emitting elements, which unlike gamma and beta particles cannot pass through the body but are deadly when taken internally. The tests came back positive for polonium-210, an alpha emitter. If Litvinenko had died sooner, the cause of death might never have been detected.[53]

After the discovery of polonium, the British police began an exhaustive effort to trace Litvinenko's movements. Traces of polonium were found at the Pine Bar, at a sushi restaurant where Litvinenko dined with Lugovoi and Kovtun on October 16, and on the seat occupied by Lugovoi on a British Airways flight from Moscow to London on October 25.[54]

At a news conference in Helsinki the day after Litvinenko's death but before the polonium was discovered, Putin said that there was no indication that Litvinenko died a violent death and that the case was being used for political purposes. Sergei Ivanov, a deputy prime minister, said Litvinenko had a "low intellect" and was inclined to provocation. "For us," he said, "Litvinenko was a nobody."[55]

Britain sent investigators to Moscow and asked to interview Lugovoi, Kovtun, and other Russians. In response, the Kremlin said that it was conducting its own investigation and asked to question a hundred people in London, including Boris Berezovsky. Six months after Litvinenko's death, the British prosecutor officially requested Lugovoi's extradition. Putin refused, saying the Russian Constitution barred sending citizens abroad for trial even though Russia had signed the Council of Europe Extradition Convention in 2001. The British, he said, should present their evidence to Moscow prosecutors and allow the Russian judicial system to decide the case. In

December 2007, Lugovoi, who was treated as a hero in Russia, was elected to the State Duma from the Liberal Democratic Party. He insisted he was being framed by MI5. In an interview in *Izvestiya,* in answer to a question about requests that he go to London for questioning, he said, "Why should I drop everything and rush off to England?"[56]

Another prominent victim was Anna Politkovskaya, who became the most important source of information for the world on atrocities by the Russian and Chechen governments in Chechnya. On October 7, 2006, she was shot four times in her apartment building after stepping out of the elevator on her floor.

Afterward, Putin tried to minimize her significance. He said her death was "a tragedy, of course," but her "influence on the country's political life was minimal."[57] Reacting in advance to the idea that the authorities had been involved, Putin said that her murder caused "much more damage to the authorities . . . than her reporting."[58]

For ten months there was no official information about the case, but in August 2007, Russian prosecutor general Yuri Chaika announced that ten people had been arrested and would soon be brought to trial. He said the killers were Chechen criminals but that the crime had been masterminded by people outside Russia to discredit the Russian leaders.[59] Putin hinted that Berezovsky had ordered the killing.[60]

By the time the trial began, in November 2008, the number of accused had been reduced to three, Ibrahim and Dzhabrail Makhmudov, two Chechen brothers, and Sergei Khadzhikurbanov, a former police major from the organized crime unit. A fourth person, Pavel Ryaguzov, a former FSB lieutenant colonel, was suspected of a leading role in the plot but was not charged due to a lack of evidence. He was tried at the same time for a different offense. A third brother, Rustam Makhmudov, the suspected triggerman, escaped abroad.

The trial lasted for three months and ended February 19, 2009, with the acquittal of all three defendants. Many thought the FSB had sabotaged the prosecution. It had leaked information about the identity of the suspects, making it possible for the triggerman to flee, and prevented investigators from seizing Ryaguzov's office computer.[61] According to *Novaya Gazeta*, it had started following Politkovskaya in the summer of 2006 but refused to say what was found.[62]

There was evidence that besides the defendants, a shadowy "second team" had also placed Politkovskaya under surveillance. On the afternoon of her death, she was shopping at the Ramstor supermarket on Moscow's Frunze embankment. A hidden video camera captured a man in jeans and a sweater and a light-haired woman in black following her down the aisle. Investigators failed to identify the couple or explain how they fit into the murder.[63]

The ties between the assassination team, the FSB, and the police were also found to be far more extensive than was first revealed. Sergei Sokolov, the deputy editor of *Novaya Gazeta,* which conducted its own investigation, testified that Dzhabrail Makhmudov was an FSB agent and that he and his brothers were recruited by their uncle, Lomi-Ali Gaitukayev, also an FSB agent who reported to Ryaguzov and was serving time in prison for the attempted murder of a Ukrainian businessman.[64] Rustam Makhmudov was able to flee the country, Sokolov said, because the FSB supplied him with false papers.[65]

In June 2009, the three defendants' acquittal was overturned by the Russian Supreme Court, which cited procedural errors. A new trial was not immediately scheduled, but *Novaya Gazeta* found evidence that Dmitri Pavlyuchenkov, the head of surveillance of the Moscow police and a witness in the first trial, had been hired by

Gaitukayev to place Politkovskaya under surveillance. He had given the assassins her address and the weapons and bullets they used to kill her.[66]

In August 2011, Pavlyuchenkov was arrested and charged with Politkovskaya's murder. He struck a deal with the prosecution: in exchange for his naming the mastermind of the crime, the charge against him was reduced from organizing the murder to involvement in it. But he never testified about the supposed mastermind or who paid for the crime. Vladimir Markin, a spokesman for the Investigative Committee, said that "Pavlyuchenkov . . . testified that he was told by Gaitukayev that the masterminds . . . were Berezovsky and [Akhmed] Zakaev."[67] Instead of life imprisonment, he was sentenced to eleven years.

Pavlyuchenkov's deal with the prosecution made it possible to cover the trail leading to the mastermind. There is no evidence to support the official story that Berezovsky was behind the crime. On June 20, 2014, five people were convicted: Gaitukayev, who recruited the gang, and his nephew Rustam Makhmudov, the gunman, received life in prison. Ibrahim and Dzhabrail Makhmudov were sentenced to twelve and fourteen years, respectively, for following Politkovskaya the day she was killed. Khadzhikurbanov received twenty years as an accomplice. None of them is likely to have known who ordered the killing.

Besides Litvinenko and Politkovskaya, other prominent political opponents of Putin were also killed. Sergei Yushenkov investigated the apartment bombings and was ready to investigate the *Nord-Ost* hostage siege, and was also a cochairman of Liberal Russia, a new political party that appeared to have a chance to become the main democratic opposition party to Putin. He was shot in front of his apartment building on April 17, 2003, just hours after obtaining the registrations needed for the party to participate in that December's State Duma elections. Mikhail Kodanev, the other leader of Liberal Russia, was tried and sentenced to twenty years in prison for ordering Yushenkov's murder. He protested his innocence and was convicted solely on the basis of the testimony of another convicted suspect, Alexander Vinnik, who made a series of contradictory claims.[68] Two years later, Igor Korolkov, investigating the case for *Moscow News,* learned that a video camera near the building where Yushenkov was shot captured two people running from the building immediately after the killing. The police collected the tape, but it was never included in the case filed against Kodanev.[69]

In July 2003, Yuri Shchekochikhin, another Duma deputy who investigated the apartment bombings, died of an unexplained illness. In his capacity as a journalist for *Novaya Gazeta,* he also investigated the case of the Grand and Three Whales furniture stores, which were founded by the father of a high-ranking FSB official and had reportedly evaded millions of dollars in import duties. He became sick after returning to Moscow from a trip to Ryazan. The illness progressed catastrophically, from peeling skin to "edemas of the respiratory system and brain," and finally death. His relatives were denied an official medical report about the cause of his illness and forbidden to take tissue specimens. At his funeral, no one was allowed to approach his body. Journalists for *Novaya Gazeta* nonetheless managed to obtain a tissue sample and send it abroad for testing, but the sample was too small and the results were inconclusive.

Another victim was Natalia Estemirova, who worked with Politkovskaya and after her death was virtually the sole surviving source of information on torture and murders carried out by the security services under Kadyrov in Chechnya. She was abducted on the street in Grozny on July 15, 2009, and driven to a wooded area in Ingushetiya and shot. In one of her last meetings with Kadyrov, he virtually foretold her death. After Estemirova criticized the policy of compelling young girls in Chechnya to wear head scarves, Kadyrov replied, "I'm up to my elbows in blood. But I'm not ashamed of this. I murdered and will murder bad people. We're fighting with enemies of the republic."[70]

The victims of political killings were usually Russians, but one was American: Paul Klebnikov, the editor of the Russian edition of *Forbes* magazine. Klebnikov wrote a critical biography of Berezovsky using information supplied by FSB general Alexander Korzhakov, Yeltsin's chief of security. At the time of his death, he was believed to be investigating the distribution of property in Moscow by the family of Luzhkov and the redivision of property in the telecommunications sphere. He was gunned down on the street on July 9, 2004.[71]

Russian authorities charged a group of Chechens with the crime, and a trial took place in 2006 in a Moscow court. The prosecutor said the killing was ordered by Khozh-Akhmed Nukhaev, a high-ranking Chechen official, who did not like the way he was portrayed in a book by Klebnikov. This explanation convinced very few people, not only because killing Klebnikov would have been an absurd overreaction but also because Nukhaev was depicted sympathetically on the whole.[72] Nukhaev disappeared before the murder, but two Chechens, Musa Vakhayev and Kazbek Dukuzov, were accused of carrying it out at his behest. As the case progressed, Sergei Sokolov, who investigated the Politkovskaya murder, added an unexpected twist. He said that Dukuzov had ties to Gaitukayev, the FSB agent who had recruited Politkovskaya's killers.[73] Dukuzov and Vakhayev were acquitted, but the Russian Supreme Court overturned the verdict and ordered a new trial. In the meantime, Dukuzov disappeared. The Klebnikov case is no longer being actively investigated.[74]

The regime did not usually use terroristic methods against its friends, but if a friend became inconvenient, he too could be eliminated, if only to prevent him from talking. Two such friends were Putin's mentor, the former mayor of St. Petersburg, Anatoly Sobchak, and Putin's reputed liaison with organized crime, Roman Tsepov.

Sobchak was the best-known Putin colleague to die under mysterious circumstances. Putin had been Sobchak's deputy, and Sobchak was familiar with the extent of Putin's corruption in the early years of Yeltsin's rule. In 2000, while campaigning for Putin in the presidential race, Sobchak freely confided that he expected to be appointed to a high-level position after his former protégé won the election.[75] On February 17, he traveled with two male assistants to the Kaliningrad oblast to campaign. On February 19, after drinking moderately at a reception, he returned to his hotel room and died. The official explanation was that he suffered a heart attack.[76]

An autopsy performed in Kaliningrad, however, suggested that Sobchak had been murdered. In the wake of this finding, a second autopsy was carried out, this time in a military hospital in St. Petersburg. According to this report, Sobchak had had a heart attack. Despite the second autopsy, the prosecutor in Kaliningrad opened an investigation into a case of "premeditated murder with aggravating circumstances." The investigation was closed after three months without a finding.[77]

In Paris, Arkady Vaksberg, an investigative journalist who knew Sobchak and met with him during the latter's two-year exile in the city, began his own investigation and learned that the two assistants who accompanied Sobchak had been treated for mild poisoning following Sobchak's death. In August 1995, a poison applied to the telephone of Ivan Kivilidi, the head of the Russian Business Round Table, killed not only Kivilidi but also his secretary, who used the same phone. Vaksberg, who had extensive forensic experience, concluded from the apparent poisoning of the bodyguards that Sobchak had also been poisoned. He suggested that Sobchak was killed when a poison placed on the bulb of his bedside lamp vaporized after the lamp was turned on. Such poisons were developed in special laboratories in the Soviet Union in the 1930s. A few months after Vaksberg's book was published, his car was blown up in Moscow. The car was empty at the time.[78]

Equally mysterious was the death of Roman Tsepov, the cofounder of a St. Petersburg security company. When Putin was deputy mayor of St. Petersburg, Tsepov regulated relations between the mayor's office and the St. Petersburg criminal world.[79] He fell ill on September 11, 2004, after drinking tea in the headquarters of the St. Petersburg FSB. He first experienced severe vomiting and diarrhea and a sharp drop in his white blood cell count, then began to lose the skin from his tongue and lips. Soon he resembled a leukemia patient who had undergone chemotherapy. When he died, on September 24, his body had a level of radiation a million times higher than normal.[80]

Tsepov's funeral was attended by high-ranking members of the FSB and the Interior Ministry as well as by his longtime business partner Vladimir Barsukov-Kumarin, the alleged head of the Tambov criminal organization. Only close friends and relatives went to the cemetery, Barsukov-Kumarin among them. A troop of policemen honored Tsepov's memory by firing into the air.

Local prosecutors opened a criminal case in connection with the death, but it was quickly closed due to a "lack of suspects." In fact there were many people who might have wanted Tsepov dead. "The self-assurance of Tsepov and the amount of information he possessed had reached dangerous proportions," wrote Vaksberg, who also made a study of this case. "Everyone also realized that his killers were present at their victim's ceremonial funeral."[81]

# 5

## A System Under Threat

The system created under Putin was oppressive but not overbearing. It demanded participation in or tolerance for corruption, but this was seen by many Russians as a minor compromise more than compensated for by the improvement in their material circumstances.

Dmitri Medvedev, Putin's longtime protégé, was elected president in 2008. In this way, Putin ostensibly respected the Constitution, which limited the president to two consecutive terms in office. Medvedev immediately made Putin his prime minister, and power in Russia never really changed hands. Putin loyalists occupied 95 percent of the positions in Medvedev's government, and Putin continued to be the real source of power. Mikhail Delyagin, the director of the Institute of Globalization, commented that Medvedev "is not capable of running anything, even his own secretariat. Putin chose the most reliable way to stay in power—the complete incompetence of his successor."[1]

For a time, Putin and Medvedev pretended to compete. Putin advocated "stable, calm development." Medvedev, in apparent response, said, "It is wrong for us to orient ourselves only to calm and measured growth. This . . . can conceal a banal stagnation."[2] He called Russia's raw material wealth a "narcotic" and denounced the country's corruption and "legal nihilism."[3] But he took no steps to deal with these problems. His statements were intended to sound presidential, but their only effect was to give false encouragement to liberals who hoped for a positive evolution.

Medvedev made one change in the Putin system during his four years as president: he succeeded in increasing the president's term from four years to six. The stability of the Putin system, however, could not last forever. The longer the regime held on to power, the more corrupt it became and the more contemptuous of limits, which put it increasingly at odds with the population. The Russian economic boom, in turn, could not go on forever. In 2008, the growth rate declined sharply as a result of the world economic crisis. It recovered in 2009 but did not return to its previous level. Lev Gudkov, the director of the Levada Center, wrote in *Novaya Gazeta* in September 2011, "A poor society that was tired of upheavals was ready to turn a blind eye to administrative caprice and the war in Chechnya, corruption and growing social inequality not to mention sham democracy and electoral sleight of hand. The overwhelming mass of people, including the poorest, believed that the increase in wealth would continue for a long time to come."[4]

The economic crisis undermined this confidence. Suddenly there were doubts about the future and a loss of faith in the authorities' ability to lead. The process that led to the political awakening of the population, however, began not with the economic situation but when Russians realized that Putin intended to remain in power for life.

In 2011, Putin started to give unmistakable signs that he intended to take back the presidency. He again became the object of fawning attention on state television, riding a Harley-Davidson motorcycle and sitting at a piano singing the 1950s hit "Blueberry Hill." Vladislav Surkov, the first deputy head of the presidential administration, confessed in an interview in July 2011 that he believed that Putin was sent to Russia by God.[5] The media reported that an all-female sect believed Putin was the reincarnation of the apostle Paul.[6]

On September 24, 2011, Medvedev officially announced at a United Russia Party congress that he would not run for a second term as president and called on the party to support Putin. Putin then announced that he intended to run. In response, Archpriest Vsevolod Chaplin, a spokesman for the Russian Orthodox Church, called Medvedev's decision to bow out an example of "kindness and integrity in politics" that should be a "source of envy" for "the majority of countries in the world," including "those that pretend to lecture us."[7]

The realization that Putin was returning to power, however, had a demoralizing effect on Russia's urban middle class, an estimated 40 percent of the population in Moscow and 20 to 30 percent in the other major cities.[8] Many began calculating how old they would be when Putin left office after two more terms, in 2024. For most, the future under Putin promised little besides professional futility and national stagnation.

On December 4, elections were held to the State Duma, and United Russia got a majority amid clear indications that the elections were falsified. In an age of cell phones, photos showing ballot-box stuffing and multiple voting poured into the headquarters of vote monitors from all over the country. The official result was 49.3 percent of the vote for United Russia, giving it 238 of the 450 seats in the Duma. But according to analysts, the party could not have gotten more than 35 percent.[9] Voters in closed institutions such as the military, asylums, and prisons were the easiest to coerce, and these voters gave United Russia overwhelming support. In one Moscow psychiatric hospital support for United Russia was 99.5 percent.[10] State employees were also pressured to vote for United Russia, and voters were able to vote repeatedly with the help of registration lists full of "dead souls."[11]

The vote counts were sent from the polling stations to the Central Election Commission, where the results for United Russia were sometimes inflated two to three times. In Moscow, one exit poll, later withdrawn for "inaccuracy," gave United Russia 27 percent of the vote.[12] When the Central Elections Commission made its announcement, United Russia's total in Moscow had jumped to 46.5 percent. Across the country, neighboring precincts showed wildly disparate returns, with some reporting 30 percent support for United Russia and others 80 percent.[13] An analysis showed that the vote for United Russia tracked in almost linear fashion with the turnout, indicating ballot stuffing in favor of the party. The results for United Russia also spiked at round values—50, 60, or 70 percent—suggesting that local officials were trying to reach preestablished targets. Similar spikes had occurred in the 2007 Duma elections.[14]

The fraud in the December 4 elections came at a time when the psychological effect of the improvement in living standards was wearing off and a large part of the population was realizing that they had been effectively disenfranchised by Putin's decision to seek a third term. Opposition rallies during the 2000s had generally attracted only a few hundred people, but the clear vote fraud in 2012 drew 10,000 to a spontaneous rally on December 5 in the Chistoprudny area of central Moscow. Most had learned about the rally through social media. The blogger Alexei Navalny had branded United Russia the "party of crooks and thieves," and that slogan appeared on hastily prepared placards.[15] That rally was followed by another on December 10, in Bolotnaya Square across from the Kremlin, that was attended by 60,000 people. On December 24, a rally on Prospect Sakharova brought out more than 100,000, protesting in subzero cold. Navalny was the most popular of the rally's speakers. "I see enough people to take the Kremlin and the White House right now," he said. "But we are peaceful people—we do not do this. But if these crooks and thieves continue to deceive us, continue to lie and steal from us, we will take back what is rightly ours."[16] That day there were also protests by more than a thousand people in St. Petersburg, Perm, Samara, Kazan, Ekaterinburg, and Novosibirsk—the largest demonstrations since the fall of the Soviet Union.[17]

The appearance of mass protests in a previously quiescent country did not pass unnoticed in the Kremlin. For eleven years, the Putin regime had built a system of bureaucratic control that, as long as the ruling group remained united, could not be challenged other than by mass protests. Now the possibility of such protests was no longer purely theoretical. Lilia Shevtsova, one of Russia's most astute analysts, wrote that the new social activism led to panic among the leadership, which feared that the loss of political control meant a loss of freedom or even life. "Lights burned late in the Kremlin," she wrote, and "conclusions were drawn: Lose your grip on power and you end up like Hosni Mubarak or Muammar Qadhafi."[18]

The calm of the Putin years masked an underlying lack of confidence, and as the protests continued, observers saw what Elena Panfilova called a "last days of Pompeii syndrome."[19] Nearly everyone who had amassed wealth had done so with political protection, and if the person conferring a monopoly was in danger, so were those who depended on his corrupt support. Leading businessmen and bureaucrats began seeking safe havens, laundering their money, and shipping their assets abroad. This had happened in 2008, when there was uncertainty over whether Putin would run for a third term, but the flight of wealth in the wake of the 2011 protests was three to four times as great. An American lawyer with close connections to the Putin era oligarchs remarked that "the lack of patriotism of the elite is astounding."

As the March 4 presidential election neared, Medvedev announced a number of reforms that were intended to defuse the protests. These included the reintroduction of the direct election of governors and an easing of the requirements for the registration of political parties. The election of governors, however, was counteracted by the government's control over nominations, and the liberalized registration was neutralized by a ban on coalitions. It mostly encouraged the creation of a myriad of Kremlin-sponsored minor parties that confused the electoral situation even further.[20]

On February 4, an estimated 125,000 people were brought to Poklonnaya Hill, the site of the memorial park commemorating the Soviet victory in World War II. The audience consisted of many state employees, who were paid bonuses to attend; migrant workers were bused in from the provinces to swell the crowd. They were told that the liberal opposition was run by the United States and NATO, and if victorious, it would hand over Russia's nuclear weapons to the United States.[21]

The presidential election, on March 4, 2012, was marred by the same falsification as the previous December's parliamentary elections. Officially, Putin received 63.8 percent of the vote. A count made by the vote monitoring organization Golos on the basis of a tally of protocol data obtained by short message service (sms) transmissions from polling places around the country, however, showed that the real figure was 50.75 percent.[22] Other experts estimated

Putin's share at 45 to 50 percent, including all the state employees paid or compelled to vote for him.[23] The difference between Putin's real vote and the reported vote may have included votes shifted from Prokhorov, who had been expected to poll well but received only 8 percent of the vote.[24] Prokhorov's candidacy was a way of controlling the outcome in any case. In an open contest, the votes cast for Prokhorov would have gone to a liberal, anti-Putin candidate.

The authorities seized their "victory" with a great show of relief. On the night of March 4, Putin gave a tearful speech in Manezh Square, next to the Kremlin, thanking his supporters.

But the vote tampering also energized the opposition. A demonstration in Bolotnaya Square took place on May 6 to protest Putin's inauguration. Between 50,000 and 100,000 people marched through the streets, but as they approached the Square, they were met by heavily armed police, who allowed only a very narrow corridor for them to enter. Demonstrators were pushed up against the police line by the pressure from behind.[25] In response, the police attacked and dozens of protestors were beaten. Some of them responded by throwing stones. Nearly 600 people were detained, and 13 were arrested, many of them apparently chosen at random.[26]

In the aftermath of the May 6 riot, Putin changed the law on meetings to include huge fines for participating in unsanctioned rallies.[27] Despite this and other measures, demonstrations continued for the rest of the year. In September, Navalny ran for mayor of Moscow, and despite a lack of funding or television exposure, he gained almost 30 percent of the vote. But the opposition had lost energy, not least because its various factions—liberals, socialists, and nationalists—lacked a coherent program other than opposition to Putin, whose support among the population was still strong. By 2013 the protest wave had largely dissipated, just as much more massive opposition was building against a regime that closely resembled Putin's in neighboring Ukraine.

In 2010, Viktor Yanukovych was elected president of Ukraine. Privatization in Ukraine was dishonest everywhere, but in the Donetsk oblast, where Yanukovych got his start, it was carried out at the point of a gun. Yanukovych owed his political career to Rinat Akhmetov, the country's richest oligarch, who began as an enforcer for Akhat Bragin, a leading Ukrainian gangster. In 1995, after Bragin and six of his bodyguards were killed in a bombing at the Donetsk soccer stadium, Bragin's financial empire was taken over by Akhmetov.[28]

In 2010, there was a democratic majority in the Verkhovnaya Rada, the Ukrainian parliament. After Yanukovych acceded to power, however, he forced deputies to ally with his Party of the Regions, using government officials and his criminal associates to threaten their businesses. Since protecting their financial interests was the reason many Ukrainian deputies went into politics in the first place, these tactics were highly successful. Once Yanukovych had secured a parliamentary majority, he used it to remake the Constitutional Court, firing six of the eighteen judges. This gave him a controllable majority. The Constitutional Court then stripped the Supreme Court of its ability to review appeals. At the same time, the judicial congress, which regulates the judiciary, shifted power to the judges of the administrative and economic courts, which were the most corrupt. In this way, Yanukovych took over the judiciary.[29]

Once he had the requisite control, he and his cronies embarked on a campaign of mass expropriation similar to what had taken place in Russia after the arrest and conviction of Khodorkovsky. Businessmen were offered below-market prices for their businesses, and if they did not accept, criminal cases were opened against them in court. Those who tried to resist the seizure often learned that they were the ex-owners of their enterprises on being handed a court decision in a case of which they had no previous knowledge.[30]

Raiding at the highest level led to raiding at the local level, creating a pervasive atmosphere of lawlessness. But unlike Russia, where there was a widespread belief that Putin is fighting corruption instead of directing it, in Ukraine there was no doubt that the person responsible for the country's new gangland atmosphere was Yanukovych himself.

As Yanukovych consolidated power in his hands, Ukrainians also witnessed the rise of his son, Oleksandr, a forty-year-old dentist who became a multibillionaire in two or three years. Yanukovych used his son as a counterweight to Akhmetov and another powerful oligarch, Dmytro Firtash. But the open promotion of Oleksandr inspired a visceral reaction against the government. At the same time, the seizure of property by the Yanukovych family and the appointment of loyal but incompetent managers to run it had a visibly damaging effect on the Ukrainian economy, which had been hard hit by the world economic crisis and never really recovered.[31]

The system that allowed Yanukovych and his cronies to engage in massive theft also led to the degradation of the Ukrainian police and prosecutors, creating a situation in which Ukrainians felt vulnerable to arbitrary arrest and imprisonment. Anger over this situation came to a head in the summer of 2013 in the town of Vradievka, in the Nikolaev oblast.

On the night of June 26, Irina Krashkova, a twenty-nine-year-old divorced bookkeeper, was walking home from a discotheque when she was abducted by two police officers and a cab driver, gang-raped and beaten with a metal rod, and left for dead. After the attack, her assailants went to get a shovel to bury her, but while they were gone she managed to crawl to safety. She then identified her attackers: Yevgeny Dryzhak, a police captain, Dmitri Polishchuk, a senior lieutenant, and the driver, Sergei Rabenenko. Only Polishchuk and Rabenenko were detained. Dryzhak, whose relatives were high-ranking local officials, was not charged, and the head of the Vradievka police and five fellow officers provided him with an alibi.[32] As news of what had happened to Krashkova spread, people started to gather in the city center. In the previous three years, the police in Vradievka had raped and killed five women, and then tortured men to force them to confess to the crimes. Three of the men had hanged themselves, and one died at home from the torture.[33] Soon there were a thousand people in the square; they stormed the police head-quarters and were dispersed with tear gas.

The riot in Vradievka inspired protests against the police in cities all over the country. On July 7, dozens of residents of Vradievka left for Kiev on foot to demand the punishment of those guilty of the rapes and murders, and the resignation of Vitaly Zacharchenko, the interior minister. After arriving in Kiev, the protestors went to the Maidan Nezalezhnosti (Independence Square), where they set up a tent camp that was broken up by the police. On July 27 there was another protest in the Maidan against police terror, and ten people were arrested. The protests eventually came to an end, but not before the entire country was aware of what had happened in Vradievka and what, in the eyes of many Ukrainians, could happen to them.

Despite anger over Yanukovych's conduct, there was a belief that he could not be challenged because he had successfully centralized power in his own hands. A series of chance events, however, turned simmering discontent into a revolution. Yanukovych presided over a totally corrupt regime, but he had given Ukrainians a glimmer of hope by promising an "opening to Europe." In November, however, plans to sign an association agreement with the European Union were unexpectedly dropped. On November 21, there began to be small-scale protest demonstrations in the Maidan, and on Sunday, November 24, approximately 100,000 people massed to call for a "European Ukraine." The Ukrainian leaders attended the EU summit meeting in Vilnius on November 28–29 but at 10 PM on November 29, it was announced that Ukraine had declined to sign the agreement and there was no mention of future talks. This created the impression that the path to Europe was permanently closed.

Most of the nearly 10,000 people who had gathered in the Maidan to support association with the EU dispersed after the announcement, but about 300 students remained. At 4 AM, they were attacked without warning by Berkut riot police and savagely beaten. Thirty of the students had to be hospitalized. Many fled to the nearby Mikhailovsky Zlattoverkhy Cathedral, the same monastery where, centuries ago, Kievans had hidden from the Mongols.

The mass beating of the students was unprecedented in post-Soviet Ukraine. In response, three opposition parties announced that they were forming a Committee of National Resistance. On Sunday, December 1, half a million people gathered in the Maidan in support of Ukraine in Europe and to protest the actions of the Berkut. That night, radicals who may have been provocateurs attacked Berkut forces guarding the presidential administration. In the "counterattack," hundreds of protestors and at least forty journalists were injured. Activists from the Svoboda and Batkivshchyna parties then broke down the doors of the trade unions building on the Maidan and claimed it as the protest headquarters.

Events now gained a momentum of their own. The demonstrators started building barricades and putting up tents in the square. They also took over a city administration building just off the

Maidan, and as many as a thousand demonstrators a night began sleeping in the columned hall.

A stage was set up in the square for speeches and performances, and the oratory of opposition leaders as well as crowd scenes were flashed on a huge screen on the trade unions building wall. Medical, security, and food services began operating, with the help of hundreds of volunteers. Everywhere there were signs: "Ukraine in Europe," "Bandits, get out," and "Ukraine without Yanukovych."

When I arrived in Kiev on December 4, the fifth day of the protest, to renew my journalistic visa, I asked the cab driver who picked me up at the station what was going on. He answered: "Revolution."

While waiting for the processing of my visa, I talked to people in the square, who gave their reasons for the uprising against Yanukovych.

Pyotr, a teacher from Kiev, said of Yanukovych, "This is a *zek* (convict), a bandit who came to power. It's a Tatar-Mongolian horde. You can't call them anything else. What he does would be not be possible in a single civilized country."

Anatoly Boiko, a pensioner from Kiev, said, "We hate this power because it is based on complete thievery. Ukraine is being emptied and they have their money in Europe and the U.S."

Alexander Reshetnyak, a welder from Lugansk, said, "I live in a village where there is no gas, no water, no medicines in the clinic, no heat. To live in this country is not possible."

Many people in the square emphasized that if the movement was repressed and people were killed, the whole country would rise up and there would be civil war.

There were always thousands of protestors in the Maidan, although their numbers rose and fell. There were also flags: blue and yellow Ukrainian party flags; blue, red, and white flags of Ukrainian political parties; European Union flags; Georgian flags; and, more ominously, the red and black flags of radical Ukrainian nationalists, as well as that of the Ukrainian National Self Defense (UNA-UNSO), which includes a symbol resembling a swastika. The UNA-UNSO flag eventually all but disappeared amid the suspicion that the members of this organization were provocateurs.

The protestors demanded that the government resign and that Ukraine sign the association agreement with the European Union. They did not, at first, demand that Yanukovych step down, but this was only because they did not see a reasonable way of removing him.

With the first snow, the encampment in the Maidan took on an air of permanence. The barricades were reinforced with heavy pipes and wooden platforms, and the entrances were narrowed to make it easier to control the flow of people. The square was covered with tents, and new ones continually went up. They included an ecumenical "prayer" tent, as well as a medical station and outdoor movie theater. In the tents, the protestors cooked and slept, keeping warm with wood-burning *burzhuika* (bourgeois) iron stoves of the kind used by troops in World War II. Outside the tents, groups of men sat on makeshift benches around rusted metal barrels where flames from burning logs gave off showers of crackling sparks.

As the weeks passed, the protest showed no sign of waning. Instead, its food services and self-defense brigades became institutionalized. The protestors' determination grew in part from desperation. Arseny Yatsenuk, the leader of the Batkivshchina Party, said in a speech that Yanukovych behaved like a personal tsar and treated people like "cattle."[34]

The difficulty for Yanukovych in resolving the crisis—if that was his intention—was that he was distrusted by nearly all elements of society. The elite hated him because they were the first victims of his seizure of property, and the ordinary people hated him because they felt they were living under the heel of a criminal organization.

On December 13, Yanukovych convened a meeting with opposition leaders. He offered amnesty and a moratorium on the use of force if the demonstrators would end the protests. But the protestors feared that their identities were being registered and that if the protest ended without achieving its goals, Yanukovych would launch mass repression. There was no agreement. As the revolt continued, with Yanukovych refusing to address the protestors' concrete demands, the demonstrators' biggest enemies became exhaustion, the need to report to work, and the onset of cold weather.

As the Christmas holidays approached, Yanukovych secured a $15 billion financial rescue package from Russia, and the crowds started to dwindle. Opposition leaders said that it might be best to focus on the next presidential election. For the first time since the protests began, the demonstrators' determination seemed to be waning.

On January 16, however, Yanukovych's allies in the parliament passed a set of laws providing for harsh fines and long prison terms for participation in protests. The new laws would have allowed the government to put every participant in Maidan in prison, and the threat of repression galvanized the demonstrators. On the night of January 19, there were bloody clashes between demonstrators and the police, and Maidan returned to the front pages of the world's newspapers.

Both sides escalated the conflict. On January 22, Dmitri Bulatov, one of the Maidan activists, was abducted. He was held prisoner for eight days, during which time he was tortured, including having his hands nailed to a door. Another activist, Yuri Verbytsky, a seismologist from Lvov, abducted from a hospital where he was being treated for an eye injury he had suffered in the Maidan, was later found dead in a forest. His body showed evidence of torture.[35] At least five other activists were also reported missing.

At the same time, Yanukovych and the ruling party lost control in the western and central regions of the country, including Kiev. On January 23, protestors in Lvov occupied the regional administration building. Demonstrators in Rivne demanded that riot police deployed to Kiev return home. In Cherkasy, thousands of protestors clashed with police protecting the municipal administration building. On January 28, in an attempt to quiet the uprising, the parliament revoked the laws on protests it had passed only twelve days earlier and Azarov and the cabinet resigned. Clashes between demonstrators and the police in Kiev declined, and the press reported that multiple nationalist factions that were independent of any political party had splintered within the movement.

On January 29, however, Yanukovych made a fatal mistake. He forced the parliament to vote for his version of an amnesty bill that made the freeing of dozens of detained protestors conditional on an end to the occupation of administrative buildings. The bill also contained an ultimatum: if the protestors failed to end the occupations within fifteen days, the police would retake the buildings by force.[36] On February 2, tens of thousands of demonstrators rallied in the Maidan to reject Yanukovych's terms. They now demanded Yanukovych's resignation and early parliamentary and presidential elections. The rapidly deteriorating political situation caused previously loyal deputies to desert the president.

On the morning of February 18, protestors marched on the Verkhovna Rada, demanding changes to the Constitution that would limit the president's power. The situation became violent after the speaker of parliament cut off discussion on the subject. The police sent in *titushki,* paid pro-government thugs, to attack the demonstrators. A group of demonstrators invaded the headquarters of the Party of Regions, setting fire to it. One person died in the flames.[37] Security forces attacked the barricades at the top of the square and advanced on the demonstrators, using water cannons, rubber bullets as well as live ammunition, and tear gas, killing three protestors.[38] Crowds tried to march on the parliament but were gunned down with automatic-weapons fire.[39] As the fighting escalated, almost eight thousand demonstrators retreated into the square and set fire to tents, mattresses, and tires to create a barricade of flames.[40] The fighting and gunshots went on all night. By morning there were twenty-five dead, including nine police officers.[41] The police said that their officers were shot in the head and neck over bulletproof vests with sniper bullets, but the shooters were never identified. It appeared that a third force armed with sniper rifles, separate from the police and the known leadership of the Maidan, was also taking part in the killing.[42] Some of the protestors were killed by firearms, others were beaten to death with truncheons by the police. In addition to those killed, hundreds were wounded on both sides.[43]

With the mass killing on the 18th, the attitude of the protestors underwent a change. Demonstrators armed themselves with bats, shields, and army helmets. The previous lightheartedness disappeared. Instead, there was almost military discipline and, everywhere, faces hidden under black balaclavas. The Maidan became an armed camp.

On February 19, demonstrators led by militant nationalist groups, including the Right Sector and the Svoboda Party, pushed past police barricades and took control of nearby streets. In Uzhgorod,

Lutsk, Khmelnitsky, and Poltava, protestors seized police stations and administrative buildings, and in Lvov they reoccupied the regional administration building.[44] The Yanukovych government declared a truce with the leaders of the opposition.

In the meantime, the SBU announced that on February 18, fifteen hundred weapons and 100,000 rounds of ammunition had been seized in raids on five district police stations in Lvov and the headquarters of the Interior Ministry's western command.[45] Rumors spread that the weapons were on their way to Kiev. But in light of the sniper attacks in the Maidan on the 18th, no one was sure in whose hands the guns would end up, or who would be shooting at whom.

On the morning of February 20, shooting broke out, and radicals smashed through the police lines established two days earlier. The protestors surged out of the square up Institutsky Street to the government district, and the police gave way, firing as they pulled back. The protestors then began to be picked off by snipers firing from the roofs and windows of surrounding buildings. The demonstrators ducked behind trees and ran for cover. The police also came under fire, and evidence uncovered later seemed to show that at least some of the snipers were firing at both protestors and the police.[46] Busloads of riot police deserted the scene and were replaced by Berkut units, which then also retreated. When the firing ceased, corpses littered the streets and the city center was firmly in the hands of the opposition. Some sixty riot police were "taken prisoner."[47]

Oleh Musiy, the head doctor for the opposition, said seventy protestors were killed, bringing the number killed in seventy-two hours to about one hundred.[48] These victims became known in Ukraine as the "heavenly hundred." According to the Ukrainian Interior Ministry, sixteen police officers were also killed in the February 20 fighting.[49]

The shock of the killings mobilized the opposition. Residents of Kiev brought food and drink to the protestors and began reinforcing the barricades, creating huge choke points around the city center. Yanukovych agreed to talks with three leaders of the opposition, mediated by the foreign ministers of Germany, Poland, and France. To protest the violence, twelve members of Yanukovych's party and the mayor of Kiev resigned.

After "a night of difficult negotiations," Yanukovych and the opposition leaders agreed on a peace deal that provided for a return to the 2004 Constitution, which shifted power from the president to the prime minister, early presidential elections, the creation of a new coalition government, and amnesty for all involved in violent rioting. Yanukovych also agreed to refrain from imposing a state of emergency and to give the protestors three days to surrender all illegal weapons.

The security forces on which Yanukovych depended for his power, however, were preparing to abandon him. Shortly after the killings in the Maidan, the Ukrainian parliament ordered all Interior Ministry troops and police officers to return to their barracks. This was viewed by police as the first step toward blaming them for the violence. Middle-level officers tried to contact their superiors but were unsuccessful. In response, police began "laying down their shields" and leaving Kiev.[50] As the European envoys left the presidential compound, security personnel were streaming out of the city, leaving the government buildings unguarded.[51]

The details of the peace agreement were announced in Maidan by the leaders of the opposition, but in light of the killings, which were overwhelmingly blamed on Yanukovych, many protestors felt it was unthinkable to compromise with him or leave him in place. The Right Sector and other activists demanded that Yanukovych resign by 10 AM and warned that if he did not, they would remove him by force.

With the presidential administration and Yanukovych's home both left unguarded, Yanukovych now feared for his life and decided to flee, flying to Kharkov. The violence that had convulsed Kiev came to a complete halt after he left. On Saturday, February 22, the streets were empty of police, and the protestors took control of the presidential administration and Yanukovych's residence simply by walking through the front gate.

In Moscow, the events in Ukraine were seen as a textbook example of the popular overthrow of a kleptocratic ruler that could be duplicated in Russia. The regime in Ukraine was almost identical to what had been created in Russia, with the sole difference being that Ukraine, with a nationalist west and center and a pro-Russian east, was more pluralistic. Under these circumstances, it was essential to the Russian leadership that the Ukrainian revolution be discredited. The regime chose the method traditionally used to distract the Russian population from their rulers' abuses. They started a war.

On February 22, the day after Yanukovych fled Kiev, Russia began planning a special operation to seize the Crimean peninsula, which had been transferred to Ukraine in 1954 by Nikita Khrushchev. In an interview for a documentary, *Homeward Bound,* produced by state-run Channel One television to mark the first anniversary of the annexation, Putin said he had made the decision at 7 AM after an all-night emergency meeting with his security chiefs on the crisis in Ukraine. He said he told his colleagues to begin working "to bring Crimea back to Russia."[52]

On the night of February 26, 120 well-trained and armed men wearing no identifying insignias seized the Crimean regional parliament building in Simferopol and raised the Russian flag over it. They also set up checkpoints in strategic locations. There was no resistance because the Ukrainian leadership feared an armed conflict could serve as a pretext for an invasion, not only of Crimea but of the entire country. With the parliament building seized, Crimean deputies on February 27 voted to dismiss the government and appointed a new prime minister, Serhiy Askyonov, a veteran of the Crimean criminal world otherwise known as "Goblin."

On February 28, troops in camouflage but without identification seized the airport in Simferopol, blocking a number of Ukrainian military units, and the road between Simferopol and Sevastopol. They were backed by civilian volunteers wearing the orange-and-black St. George's ribbon, a symbol of Russian military prowess that had been adopted by pro-Russian activists in Crimea. A Russian warship blocked the bay at Balaklava, where the Ukrainian Coast Guard was based. On March 1, a rocket unit in Yevpatoria was seized, and in Fedosiya, the unidentified troops cut off a battalion of Ukrainian marines. The "polite, green men," as the anonymous troops were called, began to seize strategic locations everywhere.[53] They worked in small groups and with light weapons, apparently confident that there would be no military resistance. The takeover of Crimea was almost effortless. It would have been a different matter if they had been resisted with heavy weapons. But everything took place without firing and without bloodshed.[54]

The new Crimean government, in the meantime, announced that it would hold a referendum on May 25 on expanding Crimea's autonomy. On March 6, the new government announced Crimea's independence, and the date of the referendum was moved up from May 25 to March 30, then to March 16. The vote was preceded by a propaganda campaign on radio and TV, with calls to participate in the referendum, a special song about it, and the publication of a newly created newspaper, *Crimea 24*, with a circulation of half a million.[55]

The official result of the referendum was 96.77 percent for Crimea becoming part of Russia, with an 83.1 percent voter turnout.[56] Leaders of the Crimean Tatar community, who rejected union with Russia, said that the actual turnout could not have exceeded 40 percent.[57] Following the referendum, the Crimean parliament declared Crimea's independence from Ukraine and asked to join Russia.

Russia justified its invasion of Crimea by saying that it needed to protect the Russian-speaking population from neo-Nazi extremists. It showed a video of "extremists in Crimea attacking Russian soldiers." It was later confirmed that the video was made not in Crimea but in Kiev, during the street battles on February 20.[58]

On March 18, 2014, Putin made a speech in the Kremlin in which he gave the version of events that would become the basis for Russian propaganda regarding Ukraine. "In people's hearts and minds," he said, "Crimea has always been an inseparable part of Russia." But history had been unjust. "Unfortunately, what seemed impossible became a reality. . . . The USSR fell apart. . . . It was only when Crimea ended up as part of a different country that Russia realized that it was not simply robbed, it was plundered." Putin said that the new rulers of Ukraine were illegitimate and that the former leaders "milked the country, fought among themselves for power, assets and cash flows and did not care much about the ordinary people." The new leaders, however, "resorted to terror, murder and riots. Nationalists, neo-Nazis, Russophobes, and anti-Semites executed this coup." He said that "the residents of Crimea and Sevastopol turned to Russia for help in defending their rights and lives. . . . Naturally, we could not leave this plea unheeded; we could not abandon Crimea and its residents in distress. This would have been betrayal on our part."[59]

On March 28, the acting president of Ukraine, Oleksandr Turchinov, bowed before superior force and issued a decree calling for the withdrawal of Ukrainian units from Crimea. The takeover of Crimea led to a surge of chauvinistic euphoria in Russia that was carefully cultivated by the Russian state-controlled media. The government sponsored celebrations of the "return" of Crimea to Russia under the slogan "Crimea Is Ours." Support for Putin reached a three-year high.[60]

The seizure of Crimea was only one part of the Russian pressure on Ukraine. In late March, Russia began to mass troops on the border with Ukraine, deploying forty thousand to fifty thousand in twenty-four hours. In early April, pro-Russian groups stormed government buildings in various oblasts in eastern Ukraine. The first wave of attacks took place on April 6, 2014. Under the cover of a crowd of demonstrators, armed men in masks seized the headquarters of the oblast administration in Kharkov, declaring the oblast independent. At the same time and in the same way, the buildings of the city administration and the SBU were seized in Donetsk, which was declared the Donetsk People's Republic. In Lugansk, masked men with automatic weapons seized the city headquarters of the SBU after taking hostages and announcing that the building had been mined. On April 7, there was an attempt to seize the administration building in Nikolaev.[61]

The April 6 actions were followed by a larger wave of attacks on April 12. Groups of well-armed men in camouflage but without insignias or other identifying signs simultaneously attacked strategic buildings in Donetsk, Gorlovaka, Druzhkovka, Kramatorsk,

Konstantinovka, Slavyansk, Krasny Liman, Artyemovsk, and Krasno-armeisk. In Krasny Liman the attack was repulsed. The attempt to storm police headquarters in Gorlovka also failed, but on April 14, the building was taken after demonstrators formed a human shield around the attackers and the police declined to open fire. In Slavyansk, fighters seized the administration building, police headquarters, and the headquarters of the SBU; in Kramatorsk, Konstantinovka, and Krasnoarmeisk, the police headquarters were seized; and in Donetsk, the chemical factory was seized by Berkut officers who went over to the side of the "rebels."[62]

On April 13, the mayoralty in Mariupol was stormed, as were the administration building in Makeevka and the police headquarters and city council building in Yenakievo. In Lugansk, the police went over to the side of the rebels. In Odessa there was an attempt to seize the SBU building.[63] The attacks took place simultaneously and were carefully coordinated. Faced with takeovers on this scale by armed separatist groups, Oleksandr Turchinov, Ukraine's transitional president, launched a full-scale "antiterror" military operation to retake the buildings and reestablish the authority of the state.

A key figure in igniting the fighting in the Donbas region was Igor Girkin (Strelkov), a Russian citizen from Moscow who is believed to be a colonel in Russian military intelligence. While serving as an adviser in Crimea after the annexation, Girkin met there with people from the Ukrainian mainland who wanted eastern Ukraine to follow Crimea's example. He recruited fifty-two volunteers and went to Slavyansk, seventy miles north of Donetsk, where pro-Russian sentiment was deemed to be strongest. He was joined there by two hundred local men, and this force seized all of the principal government buildings in the city.[64]

On May 11, the "Donetsk Republic" held a referendum on "state sovereignty" for the oblast. According to its representatives, 89 percent of the participants voted for self-rule, and there was a 75 percent turnout.[65] On May 12, Girkin declared himself "supreme commander" of the Donetsk Republic and demanded that all military in the region swear allegiance to him within forty-eight hours. All remaining Ukrainian military in the region, he said, would be "destroyed on the spot."[66] On the same day, a referendum was held in the Lugansk oblast with an announced turnout of 75 percent, of whom 96.2 percent supposedly voted for self-rule.[67] On May 22, representatives of the Donetsk and Lugansk republics signed an agreement creating the confederative state of New Russia. The separatists then announced that they planned to incorporate most of Ukraine's southern and eastern regions, including the Kharkov, Kherson, Dnepropetrovsk, Zaporozhe, and Odessa oblasts, into the new entity.[68]

At first, the insurrection in the Donbas appeared chaotic and disorganized, but this impression was deceiving. The various strike groups were led by capable professionals from the former Ukrainian police or the Russian reserve military. The cities that were attacked were not chosen at random but were important transportation nodes for railroads and highways. By holding the Slavyansk node, for example, the rebels were able to cut off supplies to the Ukrainian Army in the northeast of the Donetsk oblast. Kramatorsk had an airport with a landing strip capable of receiving Russian military transport planes. Controlling Kramatorsk made it possible to move forces to the heart of the Donbas region by air.[69]

Slaviansk quickly became the center of the insurrection. By early June, the number of fighters holed up in the city had reached one thousand, 90 percent of whom were locals. In response to attacks by

Ukrainian forces, Vyacheslav Ponomarev, the self-styled separatist mayor, said, "We will make Stalingrad out of this town."[70]

Meanwhile, the ranks of the insurgents throughout the Donbas were growing rapidly. The Ukrainian police in the Lugansk and Donetsk oblasts, including former members of the disbanded Berkut, defected en masse to the separatists. By the end of May, the Donetsk rebels had twenty-eight thousand local volunteers, many of them criminals and unemployed.[71]

These separatists were soon joined by volunteers from Russia. The state-controlled media depicted the fighting in eastern Ukraine as a crusade to protect ethnic Russians from persecution by Ukrainian Nazis, and the flow of false information on Russian television was unremitting. The overthrow of Yanukovych was depicted not as a revolt against a kleptocratic ruler but as an uprising by Ukrainian fascists intent on suppressing Russian speakers. Among the false reports intended to stoke nationalist hysteria were the story of a three-year-old boy who was allegedly tortured and crucified by the Ukrainian military in Slaviansk, a report on the raising of the levels of the Lopan and Kharkov rivers so that NATO submarines could reach Donetsk, a report on the cancellation of the May 9 World War II commemoration in Kiev and its replacement by a gay pride parade, a report that the Ukrainians had stopped selling bread to Russian speakers, and a report that Petro Poroshenko, the Ukrainian president, was preparing to make Hitler's birthday a national holiday.[72]

This coverage helped to inspire thousands of Russian military veterans to volunteer to fight. Appeals to join the "People's Guard of Donbas" were published on the internet along with telephone numbers to call in Ukraine. An enlistment office was opened in Moscow. In announcements in the social media and on various sites supporting the Donetsk and Lugansk Republics, those wishing to volunteer were told to contact the Moscow office by email or Skype. The notices said, "The canal is open—the army of Colonel Strelkov in Slaviansk and the people of New Russia wait for your help, brothers!"[73]

Enlistment offices were also opened in Voronezh and Briansk. Volunteers were told to go to Shakhti, a city in the Rostov oblast near the Ukrainian border, where they were met and given places to stay. After a screening to determine their military knowledge, the volunteers were assigned to guides, who led them over the border through safe corridors.[74]

The atmosphere was described by Nikolai Mokrousov, a contributor to the internet newspaper *Znak:* "Almost all of the people with whom I came in contact in Shakhti and on the road to Donetsk created a pleasant impression as a result of their sincerity and self-sacrifice, which we, residents of large and small cities for some reason, have lost. It was illustrative that outside the transfer apartments in Shakhti there was an entire parking lot of cars from different regions. They were there from the Kursk region and from Moscow, of course from Rostov, and there was even a new jeep from the Khanty-Mansisk region. They were all parked in front and used for the needs of the volunteers."[75]

Many volunteers had similar stories. They were not successful in their work and family life and were leaving nothing special behind. Many trained every night for months before leaving for Ukraine. They were given cards identifying them as members of the "Home Guard." At first done secretly, the recruitment operation became increasingly open. In Ekaterinburg, volunteers began to leave from the railroad station accompanied by ovations from the crowd and the blessing of a priest. On one occasion, Vladimir Zaitsev, a local priest, said, "Beat the fascist bastards and don't be afraid of anything." The volunteers then took part in a neopagan ritual in which they stood in a circle stamping their feet and, one by one, shouted "Rus!" This was followed by a command, "To the platform!"[76]

The Russians arriving in Ukraine were not just volunteers. Despite official denials, an increasing stream of active-duty Russian soldiers were sent to join the fighting. Draftees were forced to extend their tours of duty and sent to the Rostov oblast for "training." When they arrived, they were sent over the border into Ukraine. With the first shots, they realized that these were not exercises. Contract soldiers were told there could be orders that involved crossing the border. When soldiers in the Murmansk oblast asked what the basis was for this, they were told, "You have to love your motherland. Russians are dying there and you should defend them."[77] The orders to join the fighting led large numbers of contract soldiers to cancel their contracts and terminate their service, even though they were dependent on the military for a job.[78]

Russian soldiers killed in Ukraine were buried in remote cemeteries, but by the end of August, at least seventeen secret funerals had been covered in the Russian media, including several reported by the independent regional newspaper *Pskovskaya Guvernia* and other Russian media around the northwestern city of Pskov.[79] Ukrainian military representatives said, on the basis of recovered identity papers of members of the Pskov 76th Airborne Division, that the soldiers died in fighting near Lugansk.[80]

The Ukrainian media also published interviews with active-duty Russian soldiers who had been taken prisoner. The Russian defense ministry said that they were volunteers who had gone to war while "on vacation."[81] On February 15, 2015, the Ukrainians said that Russia had deployed more than thirteen thousand soldiers, up to 300 tanks, and more than 130 multiple-rocket launch systems, artillery units, and armored personnel carriers in Donbas.[82] At the same time, Russian forces shelled Ukraine from Russian territory.[83]

The military equipment that crossed the border from Russia into the southern Donetsk oblast included T-64 tanks and BM-21 Grad multiple rocket launchers. The rebels also had man-portable air defense systems, or MANPADS, which they used to shoot down Ukrainian military helicopters.[84] In early July, the Ukrainian military became aware that three Buk-M1 medium-range antiaircraft systems, also known as the SA-11, were in rebel hands. On July 14, a Ukrainian military Antonov An-26 transport plane with eight people on board was shot down over the Lugansk region. It was flying at twenty-one thousand feet, well above the range of the MANPADS.[85]

The decision of the Russians to provide the rebels with the Buk-M1 systems led to one of the worst tragedies of the war. On July 17, Malaysia Airlines Flight 17 was shot down, killing all 298 people aboard. The airliner was flying at thirty-three thousand feet in one of the busiest air transit corridors in the world.[86]

The war in eastern Ukraine attracted some Russian speakers in the region. But it could not have been fought, let alone sustained for months, without Russian weapons, soldiers, and experienced volunteers. As the war intensified, Putin's popularity rating reached 86 percent, which exceeded even the support for Russia's 2008 war with Georgia. Just as the first Chechen war distracted Russians from the hardships of Yeltsin's economic reforms and the second Chechen war from the injustices of privatization, the war in Ukraine distracted the Russian population from the real meaning of the events there and prevented them from contemplating the possibility of a Maidan in Russia.

The distraction, however, took a high toll, as both sides engaged in indiscriminate killing. The insurgents, based mainly in the towns, fired on the Ukrainian forces from positions next to schools and hospitals and between apartment buildings. The Ukrainian forces returned the fire, using Grad multiple-rocket launchers and artillery even though they were shelling populated urban areas.[87]

When the insurgents were trying to capture an urban area, they also fired on civilians indiscriminately. But the tactics of the Ukrainian Army, extensively covered for propaganda purposes on Russian television, turned residents against the Kiev government and led some to join the rebels. Vasily Budik, an adviser to Ukraine's Defense Ministry, described the approach to Anna Nemtsova of the *Daily Beast*. "First we work with massive artillery fire to clear up space and then infantry and tanks roll in," he said. "This approach has been the same forever."[88]

Russians and Ukrainians are related peoples with a shared history, a shared ancestry, and shared family ties. The war, however, has no foreseeable end. As a result of the tactics of both sides, by early 2015, approximately fifty-seven hundred people had been killed in the fighting, and more than a million had fled their homes.

# 6

## Russia's Fate

For almost twenty-five years, post-Soviet Russia tried to create the impression that it could be considered part of the civilized world, even as it sank deeper into authoritarianism and criminality. The Maidan revolution, however, shocked the Russian leaders and brought an end to the dissimulation. The West was suddenly faced not with a masquerade but with the Russia that had existed all along, that somehow had been overlooked by many Western policy makers and observers.

After annexing Crimea, Russian leaders began threatening a nuclear attack on the West. Putin said in a documentary that he was ready to put Russia's nuclear strategic forces on high alert at the time the peninsula was seized.[1] At a meeting of retired U.S. and Russian generals in March 2015, the Russian delegates said that any attempt by NATO to win Crimea back for Ukraine would evoke a nuclear response, and "the United States should understand that it would also be at risk."[2] On March 21, Russia's ambassador to Denmark, Mikhail Vanin, told the Danish daily *Jyllands-Posten* on March 21 that if Denmark carried out plans to join the NATO antimissile defense shield, Danish ships might become targets for Russia's nuclear missiles.[3]

On February 27, Boris Nemtsov, the leader of the pro-Western liberal opposition, was shot dead as he walked on the Moskvaretsky Bridge next to the Kremlin. The bridge is monitored by video and audio equipment capable, according to a former FSB colonel, of detecting "a mouse jumping out on to the roadway."[4] The monitoring is to prevent someone from placing a bomb on the bridge or firing at the Kremlin with a grenade launcher. At each end of the bridge, closed posts are manned twenty-four hours a day by officers who survey video information and a strike group that can act immediately to block any suspicious persons.[5] That Nemtsov was murdered on that particular bridge strongly suggests that the perpetrators had official protection.

Perhaps most significant, the regime has used state-run television to rally the population in support of the war in Ukraine and against the West. Putin's approval rating, 65 percent in January 2014, jumped to 88 percent after the annexation of Crimea and has remained there ever since, sustained by an onslaught of false information about Ukrainian atrocities and hostile acts by the West.[6] The nationalistic euphoria is so all-encompassing that it can be compared to Russia's patriotic intoxication in the first weeks of World War I. In a call-in show on April 16, Putin said, "If we keep the current level of consolidation in society, we will not be afraid of any threats."[7]

The Putin regime's recent actions, however, cannot disguise his government's fundamental insecurity. With the fall of communism, the Russian people received the freedom to earn money, obtain information, speak openly, and travel abroad. The political regime, however, enshrined theft and was guaranteed with the help of repeated bloody provocations. A superstructure was created, but it is held together by mendacity and greed, and although it may sustain itself for many years, it could also collapse, a victim of its own rejection of normal moral values.

As Russia faces the future, it has three serious problems: a deteriorating economy, a fratricidal war whose cost is almost certain to increase, and a moral disintegration that may leave the regime without defenders if it faces a serious challenge. Taken together these factors are more than sufficient to undermine the system's stability.

The steady rise in living standards during the 2000s led to an implicit deal between the authorities and the population. The authorities would be free to steal as long as average incomes and living standards continued to rise. The boom, however, depended on high oil and gas prices while corruption crippled normal development. When the price of oil collapsed in June 2014, Russia had no other comparable source of revenue, and Western sanctions in response to the annexation of Crimea prevented badly needed investment.

Under these circumstances there is a serious danger of social tension. In Russia today, 110 people, mostly Putin's cronies and those connected to them, control 35 percent of the country's wealth. Average household wealth has risen sevenfold since 2000, from $1,650 in 2000 to $11,900 in 2013, but median wealth among adults in 2013 was only $871.[8]

Russia in early 2015 still had an official unemployment rate of only 5.1 percent,[9] but according to the state-controlled pollster, VtsIOM, 35 percent of Russians expected their family income to fall within the next three months due to anticipated wage cuts, and 26 percent expected a family member to be laid off.[10] In 2014, food prices rose 15.4 percent.[11] In a more normal society, these developments might not be threatening, but in Russia, a weakening economy deprives the population of its most important reason for ignoring the elites' corruption. It is a measure of the government's concern that it has cut the price on vodka, despite its need for revenue in light of falling oil prices.[12] This is a clear sign that the authorities intend to use vodka to tranquilize the population.

Besides a weakening economy, the Putin regime is threatened by the consequences of the war in Ukraine, which it initiated but whose trajectory it cannot control. Russians originally believed that the invasion of eastern Ukraine could be accomplished without casualties, like the seizure of Crimea. This belief contributed to its popularity. But as the number of regular troops and volunteers killed in Ukraine continues to grow, official attempts to conceal the extent of the casualties are often revealed as absurd or ineffectual.

After the publication on the internet of satellite photos showing a quickly growing cemetery in Rostov, Russian journalists went to the site and photographed graves with the letters "NM" for *Neopoznanyi Muzhshchina* (unidentified male) on the nameplate. There were approximately five hundred such graves. Given the heavy fighting just across the border, it was reasonable to assume that the bodies were those of Russian volunteers killed in Ukraine (regular soldiers would be returned for burial to their families). The cemetery's director, however, insisted they were the corpses that had been found on the streets of Rostov.[13]

There is every likelihood that the number of deaths will increase. Russia has fought from the beginning to discredit the revolution in Ukraine so that it cannot become an example for a similar revolution in Russia. For this purpose, rebel control over parts of the Donetsk and Lugansk oblasts, with millions of impoverished people and a dysfunctional economy, is insufficient. If the fragile cease-fire in place in April 2015 is broken and there is renewed fighting, Russian forces will face a Ukrainian Army that is rapidly professionalizing and has twenty-five hundred tanks, 44 percent of them in excellent fighting condition.[14] The result would almost certainly be thousands of casualties that will be increasingly difficult for Russian propaganda to justify, particularly if the fighting spreads to areas without large ethnic Russian populations.

Finally, the regime is threatened by the moral collapse of which it itself is the principal author. To a degree that is extreme even by the standards of kleptocracies, the Russian "elite" behaves like occupiers. Vladislav Inozemtsev, a prominent economist, said, "There is not a single country in the world where officials . . . became wealthy so quickly and on such a scale [and] persons showing such a lack of professionalism achieved such successes." Russia, he wrote, "is run like an enormous corporation . . . completely dedicated to the enrichment of its managers."[15]

The "managers," in turn, are tied economically to the West and view it as a safe haven. Insofar as corrupt wealth in Russia is a product of political patronage and the political constellation may always change, Russian oligarchs and major businessmen, rather than keeping their capital in Russia, establish a second life for themselves in the West, where they keep their bank accounts, property, and families. Many spend as little time as possible in Russia.

The resentment inspired by Russia's moneyed class is aggravated by the elite's habit of conspicuous consumption. In a 2014 program about "Black Friday," the first day of Christmas shopping in London, REN-TV showed an interview with wives of three Russian oligarchs, one of whom remarked that there was no need to seek a discount on a crocodile skin coat because £50,000 was a reasonable price. The interview, which revealed other details of the women's shopping habits, was seen by 200,000 people on YouTube and evoked a wave of abusive comments, including not only personal insults but threats. One commenter wrote, "It's necessary to organize them a beautiful life with the help of Molotov cocktails. There should be terror for these bourgeois so that they go and work as slaves for the Uzbeks and Tajiks. These chickens have learned nothing from history. The French Revolution—guillotine, the October Revolution, nationalization and shootings, the Revolution of Dignity in Ukraine, 2014, the fleeing of Yanukovych and his gang. We are waiting for a continuation."[16]

Change might come to Russia through a palace coup. Putin's adventurism has led to Western sanctions that have struck directly at many of the regime's wealthiest and most powerful figures. But since a condition for becoming wealthy in Russia is cooperation with the regime and involvement in its corruption, it is unlikely that any revolt from within would lead to a qualitative improvement in the life of the country or remedy its corrosive moral, political, and economic corruption.

Democratic change in Russia could take place, however, as the result of the same type of self-organizing anticriminal revolution that took place in Ukraine. It has been argued that the Russian population is inert and Putin's hold on power is secure. But the same arguments were made about Ukraine and Yanukovych. In any case, the fate of any democratic revolt in Russia would be decided not across Russia but in Moscow, where the population has demonstrated its capacity for political action and the number of people who are middle class is more than 50 percent.

The popular revolt in Ukraine occurred and was able to sustain itself because certain preconditions had been met. The regime's lawlessness and corruption were well known. At the same time, Yanukovych's sudden refusal to sign an association agreement with the European Union, which many saw as critical to the country's future, caused widespread shock and dismay. Finally, there was a spark—the attack by Berkut riot police on student demonstrators in the Maidan, who had gathered to support a future for Ukraine in Europe.

This pattern could be repeated in Russia. In starting a war in Ukraine, Putin sought to distract Russians from the Ukrainian example's relevance to their own situation. But despite the explosion of chauvinism that followed, Russians are well aware of the corruption and lawlessness that surrounds them and are far from convinced that Putin is not involved in it. To a degree, their willingness to absolve Putin and the regime of responsibility for abuses reflects a determination not to face reality. That determination might disappear very quickly if protests gain momentum and people begin to believe that positive change is a real possibility.

One catalyst for a democratic revolt could be the 2018 presidential elections, particularly if Putin wins a fourth term as president through massive falsification. A political crisis could also erupt because of economic collapse or a military defeat in Ukraine. Under these circumstances, a democratic revolt could be ignited by a single event that, like the beating of the students in the Maidan, reminds people of their helpless situation. In February 2010, two doctors, Vera Sidelnikova and Olga Aleksandrina, a mother and daughter, were killed in Moscow when their car crashed head-on with that of Lukoil vice president Anatoly Barkov, which, according to witnesses, turned into the oncoming lane to jump the morning traffic. The incident sparked an explosion of outrage over the internet but no demonstrations. A similar event, under the right conditions, might inspire the same type of mass revolt as the rape of Irina Krashkova in Vradievka and the beating of the students in Kiev.[17]

The prospect that the regime could face a systemic crisis makes it imperative that the democratic forces in Russia recognize the importance for Russian society of a moral revolution. Frederick Douglass wrote that the essence of the slave mentality is the tendency to treat conditions that are abnormal as if they were natural. This describes much of Russian life today. In any Russian city, corruption is so routine and well developed that the participants can easily convince themselves that they are doing nothing wrong.

The Russian opposition is quick to attack corruption. But corruption is a symptom of a deeper ill, the disregard for the value of the individual by comparison with the perceived requirements of the state. An attack on corruption that does not address this underlying subservience risks removing one group of corrupt leaders and replacing them with another group that is just as bad. The war in Ukraine, at the same time, has given renewed strength to extreme Russian nationalism, and an economic downturn could increase the appeal of left-wing socialism.

The most desirable scenario for Russia would be the removal of the Putin regime in a free and fair election. Unfortunately, there is virtually no chance that that will take place. The last honest presidential election in Russia was in 1990, before the Soviet Union fell, when Yeltsin was elected president of the Russian Republic. If the Putin regime is to be denied its goal of ruling forever, it will be not through an election, which the regime will be able to control, but because popular discontent grows so massive that the police and army become unreliable and the ruling group splits, with at least one faction going over to the side of the people.

Under these circumstances, it will be important under which banners a democratic revolt occurs. Nearly all opposition forces share a theoretical opposition to corruption. What Russia needs, however, is the triumph of a consciousness capable of guiding a popular movement away from radicalism and toward a fully articulated commitment to universal values. The tendency to treat the individual as raw material for the realization of the state's ambitions made possible the triumph in Russia of communism, which tried to create "heaven on earth" at the cost of millions of lives. The same tendency led to the determination to introduce capitalism without the rule of law and Russia's total criminalization. In the event of a future upheaval, it can wreak havoc once again.

To restore respect for the individual as the foundation for a new beginning, Russia must take an honest look at its past. Because it has failed to face the truth about the crimes of the communist regime, it did not purify the moral and political atmosphere after seventy-four years of communism. Facing the truth about communism and commemorating its millions of victims remains a fundamental requirement for Russia to have a decent future.

An even more urgent necessity, however, is to face the crimes that were committed after the fall of communism, including the 1993 massacre at the Ostankino Television Tower, the shelling of the White House, the thievery that drove the privatization process, the 1999 apartment bombings, the 2002 Moscow theater siege, the 2004 Beslan school siege, the radiation poisoning of Alexander Litvinenko in London, and the murders of, among others, Anna Polikovskaya, Sergei Yuschenkov, Yuri Shchekochikhin, Paul Klebnikov, Natalya Estemirova, and Boris Nemtsov.

Of these crimes, the most important are the 1999 apartment bombings. The explosions in Moscow, Buinaksk, and Volgodonsk were the ultimate result of the country's criminalization under Yeltsin and the key to Putin's rise to power. If the Putin regime faces a democratic revolt, it will seek to defend itself by claiming it is under attack by foreign agents. The apartment bombings demonstrate that it is the Putin regime itself that is the enemy of the population, and that the regime will not hesitate to use any means at its disposal to stay in power. At the same time, the apartment bombings, more dramatically than any other episode in recent Russian history, demonstrate the inherent criminality of the Russian authorities' view that individuals exist for the benefit of the state.

It may be argued that, in the case of the apartment bombings, Putin's and Yeltsin's guilt is unproven. This is true, but only in the sense that the guilt of any criminal convicted in a court of law can be said to be ultimately unproven. The Putin regime never faced a court of law, but only because it controlled the judicial process and was in a position to seize and then hide or destroy the evidence. The totality of circumstantial evidence—which, unlike direct evidence, is impossible to fake—presents a picture of guilt so convincing that were it presented against an individual in a criminal case, the verdict would be obvious and incontrovertible. Insofar as the regime has blocked three attempts at independent inquiries of the apartment bombings and is implicated in the murders of people who tried to investigate the bombings on their own, it should be regarded as guilty. The evidence of its subsequent actions suggests that it is fully capable of these crimes. If the authorities wish to disprove allegations of their participation in the apartment bombings, they have the option of releasing vital evidence for independent examination, particularly the bomb that was planted in the basement of the building in Ryazan and was sequestered by the FSB in direct violation of Russian law, which states that evidence of extraordinary threats to the rights and security of citizens cannot be treated as state secrets.

Russia faces a darkening future. The war in Ukraine shows no signs of ending, and in the wake of the murder of Boris Nemtsov, the conditions have been created for mass internal repression. By threatening to use nuclear weapons against countries that are not Russia's enemies, the leadership has also increased the chance that they might actually be used, either through miscalculation or in a confrontation inspired by Russia's own actions. Against this, however, is the resiliency and talent of the Russian people, who succeeded, against all expectations, in overthrowing communism peacefully and who have the capacity to overthrow the new tyranny that took communism's place.

Russia's most pressing need is a truth commission, like South Africa's Commission on Truth and Reconciliation, that is able to examine dispassionately the crimes of postcommunist regimes and make them known to the Russian people. Many of these crimes were terrible, but an awareness of their true nature can be critical in building a new, democratic Russian society. In the event that Russia is able to follow the example of Ukraine in overthrowing a criminal government, it will be necessary to convene a new Constituent Assembly capable of producing a Constitution enshrining a true separation of powers. Russia has never recovered from the suppression of the elected Constituent Assembly on January 18, 1918. In its wake, political structures in Russia had no independent authority and were always used as vehicles for arbitrary power.

Russia's pro-democratic public probably amounts to no more than 10 to 15 percent of the population, but the experience of the perestroika period suggests that they can carry millions with them. To do that, however, Russia's liberals will also have to face the truth about Russia's experience of post-Soviet "democracy." Such an effort will not be easy. But it can enable the democratic forces to break with Russia's tragic history and lay a basis for the country's future. They need only to defend the worth of the individual and let truth be their guide.

# Notes

### Preface

1. Viktor Davidoff, "David Satter, the Kremlin's Bete Noire," *Moscow Times,* January 20, 2014.

2. David Satter, "Remembering Beslan," Forbes.com, October 1, 2009, http://www.forbes.com/2009/10/01/beslan-putin-politkovskaya-basaev-dzasokhov-chechen-opinions-contributors-david-satter.html.

3. Bridget Kendall, "Russia's Putin Shines at Valdai Summit as He Castigates West," BBC.com, September 20, 2013, http://www.bbc.co.uk/news/world-europe-24170137.

4. Lilia Shevtsova, *Lonely Power: Why Russia Has Failed to Become the West and the West Is Weary of Russia* (Washington, D.C.: Carnegie Endowment for International Peace, 2010), 102.

### 1. The 1999 Apartment Bombings

1. Vizit Vladimir Putin v Kazakhstan, Radiostantsiya Mayak, Novosti, September 24, 1999, cited in John B. Dunlop, *The Moscow Bombings of September 1999* (Stuttgart: ibidem-Verlag, 2012), 80.

2. Ilyas Akhmadov and Miriam Lanskoy, *The Chechen Struggle: Independence Won and Lost* (New York: Palgrave Macmillan, 2010), 162.

3. Ibid.

4. Dunlop, *The Moscow Bombings,* 80.

5. Ian Jeffries, *The New Russia: A Handbook of Economic and Political Developments* (New York: Routledge, 2002), 31.

6. Patrick Cockburn, "Russia Planned Chechen War Before Bombings," *Independent,* January 29, 2000.

7. Dunlop, *The Moscow Bombings,* 20–22.

8. "Silence After the Explosions, *Moskovsky Komsomolets,* January 19, 2000.

9. This is the opinion of Colonel General Vyacheslav Ovchinnikov, commander of Russia's internal troops. Boris Karpov, *Vnutrennie voiska: Kavazskii krest—2* (Moscow: Delovoi ekspress, 2000), 47, cited in Dunlop, *The Moscow Bombings,* 72.

10. Yuri Zakharovich, "Profits of Doom," *Time Europe,* October 6, 2003, cited in Dunlop, *The Moscow Bombings,* 73.

11. Akhmadov and Lanskoy, *The Chechen Struggle,* 157.

12. Ibid., 159.

13. Andrei Batumsky, "Sgovor," *Versiya,* August 3, 1999.

14. Vitaly Tret'yakov, "Goniteli sem'i i annibaly 'Otechestva' " *Nezavisimaya gazeta,* October 12, 1999.

15. Oksana Yablokova, Simon Saradzhyan, and Lera Kor, "Apartment Block Explodes, Dozens Dead," *Moscow Times,* September 10, 1999.

16. Dunlop, *The Moscow Bombings,* 78.

17. Ibid.

18. "Russia to Seal Off Chechnya," BBC News, September 14, 1999, http://news.bbc.co.uk/2/hi/europe/446689.stm.

19. Dunlop, *The Moscow Bombings,* 238; "September 1999 Russian Apartment Bombings Timeline," The Fifth Estate, January 8, 2015, www.cbc.ca/fifth/blog/september-1999-russian-apartment-bombings-timeline.

20. Alexander Litvinenko and Yuri Felshtinsky, *Blowing Up Russia: Terror from Within* (New York: S.P.I. Books, 2002), 75.

21. Timothy J. Colton and Michael McFaul, *Popular Choice and Managed Democracy: The Russian Elections of 1999 and 2000* (Washington, D.C.: Brookings Institution Press, 2003), 173, cited in Dunlop, *The Moscow Bombings,* 81.

22. Dunlop, *The Moscow Bombings,* 82–83.

23. David Satter, "Anatomy of a Massacre," *Washington Times,* October 29, 1999.

24. "Iz perepiski glavnogo redaktora," MK.ru, September 25, 1999, cited in Dunlop, *The Moscow Bombings,* 93.

25. Pavel Voloshin, "Chto bylo v Ryazan," *Novaya Gazeta,* February 14, 2000, http://www.novayagazeta.ru/society/11527.html.

26. Pavel Voloshin, "Geksogen. FSB. Ryazan," *Novaya Gazeta,* March 13, 2000, http://www.novayagazeta.ru/society/11303.html.

27. Dunlop, *The Moscow Bombings,* 192.

28. " 'Ryazanskii sakhar', ' s Nikolaem Nikolaevym (Sobitiya v Ryazan, September 22, 1999)," NTV, Nezavisimoye rassledovanie, March 23, 2000, https://www.youtube.com/watch?v=K-lEi_Uyb_U.

29. Alexei Levchenko and Lev Moskovsky, "Seleznev znaet, kto zryval Rossiyu," *Noviye izvestiya*, March 21, 2002.

30. Ibid.

31. https://www.youtube.com/watch?v=pfQBM2z2a5A.

32. Dunlop, *The Moscow Bombings*, 248–49.

33. Levchenko and Moskovsky, "Seleznev znaet."

34. Alex Godfarb with Marina Litvinenko, *Death of a Dissident* (New York: Free Press, 2007), 265–66, cited in Dunlop, *The Moscow Bombings*, 251.

35. Andrei Piontkovsky, "Rassledovanie: Priznanie Oligarkha Prokuroru Respubliki," *Novaya Gazeta*, January 21, 2001.

36. Igor Korol'kov, "Fotorobot ne pervoi svezhosti," *Moskovskie novosti*, November 11, 2003, cited in Dunlop, *The Moscow Bombings*, 127.

37. Ibid.

38. Dmitri Pavlov, "Zayavil nachal'nik UFSB v godovshchinu vzryva na Gur'yanove," *Kommersant*, September 8, 2000, cited in Dunlop, *The Moscow Bombings*, 94.

39. Korol'kov, "Fotorobot ne pervoi svezhosti," cited in Dunlop, *The Moscow Bombings*, 127.

40. Ibid.

41. Testimony of David Satter, "Russia: Rebuilding the Iron Curtain," U.S. House of Representatives, Committee on Foreign Affairs, May 17, 2007, http://www.russialist.org/archives/2007-115-26.php.

42. Russian Federation: Law of the Russian Federation from 21 July 1993 No. 5485-1, "On State Secrets" (with changes entered through the federal law No. 377-F3 of 21 December 2013); WIPO: World Intellectual Property Organization, http://www.wipo.int/wipolex/en/text.jsp?file_id=330101.

## 2. Yeltsin: Chaos and Criminality

1. David Satter, *Darkness at Dawn: The Rise of the Russian Criminal State* (New Haven: Yale University Press, 2003), 46; Glenn Eldon Curtis, *Russia: A Country Study* (Washington, D.C.: Library of Congress, Federal Research Division, 1998), 313.

2. Anders Aslund, "Tri Osnovye Istochniki Bogatstva Novykh Russkikh," *Izvestiya*, June 20, 1996.

3. Ibid.

4. Ibid.

5. Valeriya Bashkirova, Alexander Solovyev, and Vladislav Dorofeev, *Geroi 90-x: Lyudi i Den'gi, Noveishaya Istoriya Kapitalisma v Rossii* (Moscow: Kommersant and ANF, 2012), 101.

6. Ibid., 102.

7. Ibid., 103.

8. Ibid., 100.

9. Ibid., 102.

10. Svetlana Glinkina, "The Criminal Components of the Russian Economy," working paper no. 29, *Berichte des Bundesinstituts fur Ostwissenschaftliche und Internationale Studien,* 1997.

11. Bill Browder, *Red Notice: How I Became Putin's No. 1 Enemy* (London: Bantam, 2015), 57.

12. Svetlana Glinkina, Andrei Grigoriev, and Vakhtang Yakobidze, "Crime and Corruption," in *The New Russia: Transition Gone Awry,* ed. Lawrence R. Klein and Marshall Pomer (Stanford, Calif.: Stanford University Press, 2000), 247.

13. Bashkirova et al., *Geroi 90-x,* 116.

14. Ibid., 114.

15. "Privatization, Russian-Style," *Nezavisimaya Gazeta—Politekonomiya,* Johnson's Russia List, April 17, 2001. Between 1990 and 1998, Russia sold more enterprises than any country in the world but was in twentieth place in terms of revenue. Even Hungary, where the state controlled much less than in Russia, earned $2.1 billion more than Russia did. In Russia, privatization revenue was $54.60 per capita, compared with $2,560.30 in Australia and $1,252.80 in Hungary.

16. Bashkirova et al., *Geroi 90-x,* 167.

17. Peter Reddaway and Dmitri Glinski, *The Tragedy of Russia's Reforms: Market Bolshevism Against Democracy* (Washington, D.C.: United States Institute of Peace Press, 2001), 249.

18. Stephen Shenfield, "On the Threshold of Disaster: The Socio-Economic Situation in Russia," *Johnson's Russia List,* July 2, 1998; Murray Feshbach, "Russia's Population Meltdown," *Wilson Quarterly,* Winter 2001.

19. Ibid.

20. Shenfield, "On the Threshold"; Feshbach, "Russia's Population."

21. David E. Hoffman, *The Oligarchs: Wealth and Power in the New Russia* (New York: Public Affairs, 2011), 412.

22. Bashkirova et al., *Geroi 90-x,* 185.

23. Ian Jeffries, *The New Russia: A Handbook of Economic and Political Developments* (New York: Routledge, 2002), 31; Renfrey Clarke, "Russian Miners Demand: 'Yeltsin Out,' " *Green Left Weekly,* June 19, 1998.

24. Larisa Kislinskaya, "Kto otvetit za bazaar?" *Sovershenno Sekretno,* April 1, 2006.

25. R. C. Gupta, *Collapse of the Soviet Union* (Meerut: KRISHNA Prakashan Media, 1997), 132.

26. Reddaway and Glinski, *The Tragedy of Russia's Reforms,* 249.

27. David Satter, *Age of Delirium: The Decline and Fall of the Soviet Union* (New Haven: Yale University Press), 398.

28. Hoffman, *The Oligarchs,* 202.

29. Satter, *Age of Delirium,* 405.

30. Ibid.

31. Y. M. Baturin et al., *Epokha El'tsina: ocherki politicheskoi istorii* (Moscow: Vagrius, 2001), 353.

32. Satter, *Age of Delirium,* 405.

33. Daniel S. Treisman, *After the Deluge: Regional Crises and Political Consolidation in Russia* (Ann Arbor: University of Michigan Press, 1999), 35.

34. Aleksandr Tarasov, "Provokatsiya: Versiya sobitii 3–4 Oktyabrya 1993 v Moskve," *Skepsis,* October 20–November 13, 1993, http://scepsis.net/library/id_2571.html.

35. Leonid Proshkin, "Shturm kotorogo ne bylo," *Sovershenno Sekretno,* no. 9, 1998.

36. Ibid.

37. Satter, *Age of Delirium,* 409.

38. Ibid.

39. Proshkin, "Shturm kotorogo ne bylo."

40. David Satter, "Yeltsin: Shadow of a Doubt," *National Interest,* Winter 1993–94, 52.

41. Sergei Grigoriants, "Napravo krugom marsh . . .," grigoryants.ru, October 4, 2013, http://grigoryants.ru/sovremennaya-diskussiya/chuma-na-oba-vashix-doma.

42. Satter, *Age of Delirium,* 408–9; A. Kramer, "The Role of the Masses During the October 1993 Moscow Rebellion," Marxist.com, October 6, 2003, http://www.marxist.com/1993-moscow-rebellion-masses.htm.

43. Proshkin, "Shturm kotorogo ne bylo."

44. Reddaway and Glinski, *The Tragedy of Russia's Reforms,* 432.

45. There seems to have been a decision to force through adoption of the draft constitution at any price. In a change from the existing law on referendums intended for the adoption of decisions on constitutional questions, which required a yes vote by more than 50 percent of eligible voters—a threshold in force the previous April in the referendum on trust in Yeltsin and his economic policies—the threshold for the approval of the new constitution was set at 50 percent of actual voters, with a minimum turnout of 50 percent of those who were eligible. The threshold for approval was thus dropped from 50 percent of eligible voters to 25 percent. To justify this change, which was a direct violation of the law, the referendum was called not a referendum but "national voting." M. McFaul and N. Petrov, eds., *The Political Almanac of Russia, 1997,* vol. 1, *Elections and Political Development* (Moscow: Carnegie Endowment for International Peace, 1998), 180.

46. Matt Bivens, "Ballot Fraud: Not If, but How Much," *Moscow Times,* June 4, 1996.

47. Western observers were barred from the Central Election Commission (CEC) headquarters during the vote count. Official results were published not within ten days of the voting, as required by law, but more than two months later. They were then published only partially. After Sobyanin's finding that the turnout had been falsified by nine million votes was published in *Izvestiya,* Sobyanin's team was barred from its offices and its archives were confiscated. Bivens, "Ballot Fraud."

48. Carlotta Gall and Thomas de Waal, *Chechnya: Calamity in the Caucasus* (New York: New York University Press, 1998), 161, cited in John B. Dunlop, *The Moscow Bombings of September 1999* (Stuttgart: ibidem-Verlag, 2012), 14.

49. Simon Shuster, "Rewriting Russian History: Did Boris Yeltsin Steal the 1996 Presidential Election?" *Time,* February 24, 2012.

50. Dmitri Vinogradov, "Kak Zyuganov sdal svoikh izbiratelei i pobedu v 1996," interview with Viktor Ilyukhin, gazeta.ru, November 11, 2011, http://igpr.ru/node/1806.

51. Ibid.

52. Shuster, "Rewriting Russian History."

53. Igor Malkov, "Prodavets 'Razrezhennyi Vozdukh': Den'gi Mozhet Byt ne Tol'ko 'Derevyannyie' no Tozhe 'Berezovskyi' " *Moskovsky Komsomolets,* July 31, 1997.

54. David Satter, *Darkness at Dawn,* 56–57.

55. Bashkirova et al., *Geroi 90-x,* 252; Satter, *Darkness at Dawn,* 133–34.

56. Bashkirova et al., *Geroi 90-x,* 254; Satter, *Darkness at Dawn,* 135.

57. Satter, *Darkness at Dawn,* 186–92.

58. Rassledovanie, "Poslednyaya Zhertva Solonika," *Express Gazeta,* no. 20, 1997; Georgy Rozhnov, "Osobye Primety: Krasivaya i Molodaya," *Kriminalnaya Khronika,* March 1998.

59. Marc Bennetts, "Faith Healer Anatoly Kashpirovsky: Russia's New Rasputin," *Observer,* June 6, 2010.

60. Ibid.

61. Satter, *Darkness at Dawn,* 228–29.

62. David Satter, "A Low, Dishonest Decadence," *National Interest,* Summer 2003, 124.

63. Satter, *Darkness at Dawn,* 225.

64. Bashkirova et al., *Geroi 90-x,* 130.

65. Satter, "A Low, Dishonest Decadence," 121.

66. Roy Medvedev, *Kapitalism v Rossii?* (Moscow: Prava Cheloveka, 1998), 205–7. The World Health Organization considers that if per capita consumption of alcohol in a country exceeds eight liters (about eight and a half quarts), each additional liter subtracts eleven months from the life expectancy of the average male and four months from the life expectancy of the average female. In Russia, per capita alcohol consumption reached sixteen liters. Ibid.

67. Satter, *Darkness at Dawn,* 254.

68. Ada Gorbacheva, "Poka Nadeyus—Dyshu," *Nezavisimaya Gazeta,* January 26, 2001.

## 3. The Power Vertical

1. For a description of the ordeal of the *Kursk,* see David Satter, *Darkness: The Rise of the Russian Criminal State* (New Haven: Yale University Press, 2003), 5–23, 257–59.

2. Valeriya Bashkirova, Alexander Solovyev, and Vladislav Dorofeev, *Geroi 90-x: Lyudi i Den'gi, Noveishaya Istoriya Kapitalisma v Rossii* (Moscow: Kommersant and ANF, 2012), 30.

3. Helen Womack, "Return of the KGB," *Newsweek,* November 24, 2003.

4. "Political Trading Cards," *Exile,* October 1, 2001, http://exile.ru/articles/detail.php?ARTICLE_ID=15035&IBLOCK_ID=35.

5. Andrei Illarionov, Testimony Before the U.S. House of Representatives Committee on Foreign Affairs, February 25, 2009.

6. Roy Medvedev, *Vremya Putina?* (Moscow: Prava Cheloveka, 2001), 187.

7. Roy Medvedev, *Vladimir Putin: chetire goda v Kremle* (Moscow: Vremya, 2004), 306.

8. The INDEM think tank, founded in October 1997 by Georgy Satarov, a former adviser to Boris Yeltsin, does independent sociological research.

9. Elena Panfilova, interview with author, June 27, 2011.

10. David E. Hoffman, *The Oligarchs: Wealth and Power in the New Russia* (New York: Public Affairs, 2011), 481–83.

11. Speaking at the Kennan Institute in Washington in October 2000, Igor Malashenko, the deputy director of Media Most, the parent company of NTV, confirmed that the "Ryazan sugar" broadcast had served as a key irritant in the company's relations with the FSB and with the Russian government. Information Minister Mikhail Lesin, he said, had told him on several occasions that by airing that show NTV "crossed the line and that we were outlaws in their eyes." John B. Dunlop, *The Moscow Bombings of September 1999* (Stuttgart: ibidem-Verlag, 2012), 196–97.

12. Ben Judah, *Fragile Empire: How Russia Fell in and out of Love with Vladimir Putin* (New Haven: Yale University Press, 2013), 45.

13. Richard L. Palmer, Testimony Before the U.S. House of Representatives Banking and Financial Services Committee, September 21, 1999; David Satter, *Russia's Looming Crisis* (Philadelphia: Foreign Policy Research Institute, 2012).

14. Panfilova, interview with the author, June 17, 2011.

15. Judah, *Fragile Empire,* 64.

16. Ibid., 66.

17. Ibid.

18. "Russia's Raiders," *BusinessWeek,* June 5, 2008.

19. Ibid.; "Spasti biznes ot repressiy: Kazhdyy biznesmen—vor?" *Moscow News,* January 17, 2012.

20. Sergei Kanev, "Kak ustroeni 'kryshi' v Rossii," *Novaya Gazeta,* October 22, 2007.

21. Lilia Shevtsova, "The End of Putin's Era: Domestic Drivers of Foreign Policy," in *U.S.-Russian Relations: Is Conflict Inevitable?,* publication of Hudson Institute study group, June 26, 2007; Satter, *Russia's Looming Crisis,* 12–14; Karen Dawisha, *Putin's Kleptocracy: Who Owns Russia?* (New York: Simon and Schuster, 2014), 280–85; Anders Aslund, "Putin's Lurch Toward Tsarism and Neoimperialism: Why the United States Should Care," *Demokratizatsiya,* 2008, 20–21. The total capitalization of the Russian stock market in 2007 was $1 trillion, the same as Russia's GDP. Anders Aslund, *Russia's Capitalist Revolution: Why Market Reform Succeeded and Democracy Failed* (Washington, D.C.: Peterson Institute for International

Economics, 2007), 279. The total capitalization of just three state-run companies, Gazprom, Rosneft, and Russian Railways, is $380 billion.

22. Anders Aslund, "Unmasking President Putin's Grandiose Myth," *Moscow Times,* November 28, 2007. According to Vladimir Milov and Boris Nemtsov, while Medvedev was the head of Gazprom, 6.3 percent of the shares, worth $20 billion, disappeared. Boris Nemtsov and Vladimir Milov, "Putin: The Bottom Line," trans. David Essel, reprinted in www.larussophobe.com, March 31, 2008, https://larussophobe.wordpress.com/2008/03/31/boris-nemtsovs-white-paper-in-full/.

23. Boris Nemtsov and Leonid Martynyuk, "Winter Olympics in the Sub-Tropics: Corruption and Abuse in Sochi," trans. Catherine A. Fitzpatrick, *Interpreter,* December 6, 2013.

24. Boris Nemtsov and Vladimir Milov, *Putin: What Ten Years of Putin Have Brought: An Independent Expert Report,* trans. David Essel (Moscow: Solidarnost, 2010), 5.

25. Luke Harding, "Putin, the Kremlin Power Struggle, and the $40 bn Fortune," *Guardian,* December 21, 2007.

26. Vladimir Kara-Murza, "Stealing the Vote: The Kremlin Fixes Another Election," *World Affairs,* September–October 2011; Vladimir Kara-Murza, "Russia's Rigged Election," *Wall Street Journal Europe,* June 28, 2011.

27. Satter, *Russia's Looming Crisis,* 9.

28. Bill Bowring, "Judicial Independence in Russia," *EU-Russia Review,* no. 1, May 2006, 33.

29. Ibid.; Guy Chazan, "In Russia's Courts, a Judge Speaks Up and Gets Fired," *Wall Street Journal,* August 5, 2004.

30. Guy Chazan, "In Russia's Courts, a Judge Speaks Up and Gets Fired," *Wall Street Journal,* August 5, 2004.

31. Ibid.

32. Ibid.

33. Ibid.

34. *Russia, Press Country Profile,* European Court of Human Rights, July, 2014, http://www.echr.coe.int/Documents/CP_Russia_ENG.pdf.

35. "Minister yustitsii Alexander Konovalov: uvazehnie k zakonu v povsednevnoi zhizni v Rossii ne bylo nikogda," http://polit.ru/article/2008/06/02/interview/.

## 4. Selective Terror

1. Peter Baker and Susan Glasser, *Kremlin Rising* (New York: Scribner, 2005), 142.

2. John B. Dunlop, *The 2002 Dubrovka and 2004 Beslan Hostage Crises: A Critique of Russian Counter-Terrorism* (Stuttgart: ibidem-Verlag, 2006), 131–34.

3. Vesselin Nedkov and Paul Wilson, *57 Hours: A Survivor's Account of the Moscow Hostage Drama* (Toronto: Viking Canada, 2003), 187.

4. Ibid., 188.

5. "Chto eto bylo? Spasenie Zalozhnikov ili Unichtozhenie Terroristov," *Novaya Gazeta,* no. 86, November 21, 2002; Irina Bogoran and Andrei Soldatov, "Nepravda," *Versiya,* November 4–10, 2002; David Satter, "Death in Moscow," National Review Online, October 29, 2002; "Why Were Doctors in the Dark?" editorial, *Moscow Times,* October 28, 2002.

6. Garbielle Tetrault-Farber, "No Closure for Victims of Theater Hostage Crisis, 12 Years On," *Moscow Times,* October 22, 2014.

7. Alexander Podrabinek, "Politika na Krovi," *Prima News,* November 5, 2002.

8. Pavel Felgenhauer, "Putinskaya operatsiya spaseniyu zalozhnikov vyzivaet mnogo voprosov," Inopressa.ru, trans. and rpt. from *Wall Street Journal,* November 1, 2002; "Why Were Doctors in the Dark?"; Galina Mursalieva, "Ubival ne tol'ko gaz—Ubivalo Vremya," interview with Alexander Shabalov, director, Moskovsky Sluzhbi Spasenie, *Novaya Gazeta,* November 4–10, 2002; "Chto eto bylo?"

9. Fred Weir, "Gas Clouds Moscow Rescue," *Christian Science Monitor,* October 28, 2002; Nedkov and Wilson, *57 Hours,* 212; Bogoran and Soldatov, "Nepravda"; Oliver Bullough, "Putin Vows No Deal with 'Terrorists' After Siege," Reuters, October 28, 2002.

10. Dunlop, *Hostage Crises,* 103.

11. Ibid., 115–18.

12. Ibid., 117.

13. Anne Nivat, "Chechnya: Brutality and Indifference," crimesofwar.org, January 6, 2003, cited in Dunlop, *Hostage Crises,* 121.

14. Yuri Shchekochikin, "Nezamechennye novosti nedeli kotorye menya udivili," *Novaya Gazeta,* no. 4, January 20, 2003, cited in Dunlop, *Hostage Crises,* 123.

15. Alexandr Khinshtein, "Chernye vdovy pod 'kryshei' Petrovki," *Moskovsky Komsomolets,* July 23, 2003, cited in Dunlop, *Hostage Crises,* 123.

16. Dunlop, *Hostage Crises,* 36.

17. Ibid., 138.

18. Ibid., 144.

19. Ibid., 146.

20. Svetlana Gubareva, Karina Moskalenko, and Olga Mikhailova, " 'Nord-Ost,' Gaz ne spasal ot vzriva," *Novaya Gazeta,* March 21, 2005.

21. Nedkov and Wilson, *57 Hours*, 113.

22. Svetlana Gubareva, "Vystuplenie na press konferentsii k tretei godovshchine, 'Nord Ost' Tragediya na Dubrovke," Zalozhniki.ru, October 25, 2005, http://www.zalozhniki.ru/comment/97181.html.

23. Dunlop, *Hostage Crises*, 107.

24. David Satter, *Russia's Looming Crisis* (Philadelphia: Foreign Policy Research Institute, 2012), 28.

25. Dunlop, *Hostage Crises*, 29–36.

26. Timothy Phillips, *Beslan: The Tragedy of School No. 1* (London: Granta Books, 2007), 118.

27. Ibid., 85–88.

28. Doklad deputatskoi komissii Parlamenta RSO-Alaniya po rassmotrenniyu I vyyaneniyu obstoyatel'stv, svyannikh s tragicheskimi sobitiyami v g. Beslan 1–3 Sentyabrya 2004 goda, 18–19, available at http://www.pravdabeslana.ru/dokl.htm.

29. Ibid., 16.

30. Dunlop, *Hostage Crises*, 55.

31. Phillips, *Beslan*, 118.

32. Doklad, 7.

33. Dunlop, *Hostage Crises*, 75.

34. Spravka, "Zakhvat shkoli v Beslane. Khronika sobitii," Grani.ru, September 4, 2004, http://www.grani.ru/Events/Terrror/m.76331.html.

35. Akhmed Zakaev, interview with author, September 3, 2014.

36. Ibid.

37. David Satter, "Remembering Beslan," Forbes.com, October 1, 2009; Marina Litvinovich, "The Truth About Beslan," Pravdabeslana.ru, August 28, 2006, http://www.pravdabeslana.ru/truth.htm.

38. David Satter, "Remembering Beslan"; David Satter, "The Truth About Beslan," *Weekly Standard*, November 13, 2006; Dunlop, *Hostage Crises*, 17.

39. Vladimir Voronov, "No One Bargains with Terrorists, Do They? Beslan 10 Years Later," trans. Irina Sadokha and David Satter, Russian Studies Centre, Henry Jackson Society, in cooperation with the Russian Service, Radio Liberty, October, 2014, http://henryjacksonsociety.org/2014/09/19/no-one-bargains-with-terrorists-do-they-beslan-10-years-later/.

40. Dunlop, *Hostage Crises*, 99. There were also 784 injured. Of 1,128 hostages, only 82 emerged unharmed. Lidiya Grafova, "Chtoby nigde inikogda," *Novaya Gazeta*, August 29, 2005.

41. "Putin ne doekhal do razrushennoi shkoly," *Kavkazskii Uzel,* September 5, 2004, http://www.kavkaz-uzel.ru/articles/61146/.

42. Dunlop, *Hostage Crises,* 98.

43. Elena Milashina, "Agentura vyshla uz-pod kontrolya. i Dosha do Beslana," *Novaya Gazeta,* August 31, 2009.

44. Ibid.

45. "Shamil Basaev: 'U nas est mnogo, chto rasskazat' po Beslanu ...' " Kavkazcenter.com, August 31, 2005, http://www.kavkazcenter.com/russ/content/2005/08/31/37225/shamil-basaev-u-nas-est-mnogo-chto-rasskazat-po-beslanu—.shtml.

46. Lidiya Grafova, "Chtoby nigde i nikogda," *Novaya Gazeta,* August 29, 2005.

47. Ibid.

48. Lidiya Grafova, "Nado zhe Komu-to Verit," *Novaya Gazeta,* September 15, 2005.

49. Ibid.

50. Ilyas Akhmadov and Miriam Lanskoy, *The Chechen Struggle: Independence Won and Lost* (New York: Palgrave Macmillan, 2010), 227–29.

51. Steve LeVine, *Putin's Labyrinth: Spies, Murder, and the Dark Heart of the New Russia* (New York: Random House Trade Paperbacks, 2009), 140.

52. Ibid., 142.

53. Yuri Felshtinsky and Vladimir Pribylovsky, *The Corporation: Russia and the KGB in the Age of President Putin* (New York: Encounter, 2008), 487.

54. Ben Fenton, John Steele, Roger Highfield, and Duncan Gardham, "Net Tightens on the Amateur Assassins," *Telegraph,* December 1, 2006; LeVine, *Putin's Labyrinth,* 145.

55. "Sergei Ivanov: Litvinenko ne byl razvedchikom," www.ntv.ru, December 16, 2006, http://www.ntv.ru/novosti/99953/.

56. "Biznesmen Andrei Lugovoy—o 'delo Litvinenko': 'Pochemu Ya dolzhen vsye brosat I nestis' v Angliyu?' " *Izvestiya,* February 26, 2007, http://izvestia.ru/news/322026.

57. LeVine, *Putin's Labyrinth,* 119.

58. Amy Knight, "Who Killed Politkovskaya?" *New York Review of Books,* no. 17, November 6, 2008.

59. Ibid.

60. Ibid.

61. David Satter, "Journalism of Intimidation," Forbes.com, July 7, 2009, http://www.forbes.com/2009/07/07/paul-klebnikov-murder-opinions-david-satter. html

62. "Operativnaya soprovozhdenie ubiistva," *Novaya Gazeta,* no. 74 ot, October 6, 2008; Ilya Donskikh, "Moskva. Sostoyalas' press-konferentsiya, nosvyashchennaya zavershivshemusya sudebnomu razbiratel'stvu po delu ob ubiistve Anni Politkovskoi i opravdatel'nomu verdiktu prisazhnikh, vynesennomu segodnya," *Novaya Gazeta,* no. 17 ot, February 18, 2009; Philip P. Pan, "3 Acquitted in Killing of Russian Reporter," *Washington Post,* February 20, 2009.

63. Luke Harding, "Anna Politkovskaya Trial: The Unanswered Questions," *Guardian,* February 19, 2009.

64. David Satter, "Who Murdered These Russian Journalists?" Forbes.com, December 26, 2008, http://www.forbes.com/2008/12/24/russian-journalists-killed-oped-cx_ds_1226satter.html.

65. Charles Clover, "A Death Retold," *Financial Times,* February 19, 2009.

66. "Delo Anni Politkovskoi: Zakazchik poka 'neprikasaemii,'" *Novaya Gazeta,* December 12, 2012.

67. Ibid.

68. Genri Reznik: Kodaneva ogovorili, Grani.ru, March 17, 2004, http://grani. ru/Politics/Russia/m.63911.html.

69. David Satter, "Who Killed Litvinenko," *Wall Street Journal,* November 27, 2006.

70. "Natalya Estemirova Kidnapped in Grozny, Found Dead in Ingushetiya," *Eurasia Daily Monitor,* May 16, 2009.

71. Igor Korol'kov, "U nego ne bylo shansov vyzhit'," Svoboda.org, July 20, 2014, http://www.svoboda.org/content/article/25462059.html#page=1.

72. Ibid.

73. Satter, "Journalism of Intimidation."

74. Ibid.

75. Masha Gessen, *The Man Without a Face* (New York: Riverhead, 2012), 142.

76. Felshtinsky and Pribylovsky, *The Corporation,* 461.

77. Gessen, *The Man Without a Face,* 143.

78. "Sobchak byl otravlen po prikazu Putina—Frantsuskoe izdanie Slate," www. anticor.com.ua, October 5, 2014, http://antikor.com.ua/articles/15438-sobchak_byl_otravlen_po_prikazu_putina_-_frantsuzskoe_izdanie_slate.

79. Karen Dawisha, *Putin's Kleptocracy: Who Owns Russia?* (New York: Simon and Schuster, 2014), 77.

80. Ibid., 80.

81. Ibid.

## 5. A System Under Threat

1. Quoted in David Satter, "Putin in Charge," *Wall Street Journal Europe,* December 13, 2007.

2. "Putin: Russia Must Be Strong To Withstand Foreign Threats," Radio Free Europe/ Radio Liberty, April 21, 2011; Geoffrey T. Smith, "Medvedev Puts Russia in a Choice Situation," *Wall Street Journal,* June 23, 2011.

3. Quoted in David Satter, *Russia's Looming Crisis* (Philadelphia: Foreign Policy Research Institute, 2012), 6.

4. Lev Gudkov, "Who Is to Blame for Things Going Badly for Us?" *Novaya Gazeta,* September 21, 2011.

5. Tom Washington, "God Sent Putin to Russia, Claims Surkov," *Moscow News,* November 7, 2011, http://www.themoscownews.com/politics/20110711/188830057.htm.

6. Andrew Osborn, "All-Female Sect Worships Vladimir Putin as Paul the Apostle," *Telegraph,* May 12, 2011.

7. "V Tserkvi blagoslovit reshenie o 'mirnoi i druzheskoi' peredache vlasti ot Medvedev k Putinu," Interfax, September 26, 2011.

8. Charles Clover, "Russia's Middle Class Finds Its Feet," *Financial Times,* December 12, 2011.

9. Ben Judah, *Fragile Empire: How Russia Fell in and out of Love with Vladimir Putin* (New Haven: Yale University Press, 2013), 233.

10. Ibid. 233.

11. Ibid., 232.

12. Ibid., 234.

13. Ibid., 233.

14. Ibid., 233; Sergei Shpilkin, "Statistikii Isledovala Vybory," Gazeta.ru, December 10, 2011, http://www.gazeta.ru/science/2011/12/10_a_3922390.shtml.

15. Judah, *Fragile Empire,* 235.

16. Ibid., 243.

17. Ibid., 242.

18. Lilia Shevtsova, "Putinism Under Siege: Implosion, Atrophy, or Revolution," *Journal of Democracy,* July 2012.

19. Quoted in Julia Ioffe, "Net Impact: One Man's Cyber-Crusade Against Russian Corruption," *New Yorker,* April 4, 2011.

20. David Satter, "Russia's Choice," *National Review,* July 30, 2012.

21. Judah, *Fragile Empire,* 244.

22. Satter, "Russia's Choice"; Preliminary report, Association GOLOS—Domestic Monitoring of Elections of the President of the Russian Federation, www. golos.org, March 4, 2012, https://www.ndi.org/files/Golos-Prelim-Report-030512-ENG.pdf.

23. Satter, "Russia's Choice."

24. Fiona Hill and Clifford G. Gaddy, *Mr. Putin: Operative in the Kremlin* (Washington, D.C.: Brookings Institution Press, 2013), 356.

25. Satter, "Russia's Choice."

26. Ibid.

27. Ibid.

28. Denys Kazanskyi, "Akhmetov's Losing Bet," *Ukrainian Week,* May 18, 2015.

29. David Satter, "Kuda ukhodit ukrainskii oligarkh," *Kievsky dnevnik* chast' 3, Svobodanews.org, December 10, 2013, http://www.svoboda.mobi/a/us-terror-threat/25196402.html.

30. Ibid.

31. David Satter, "Krizis i Sem'ya Yanukovycha," *Kievsky dnevnik* chast'4, Svoboda.org, December 14, 2013, http://www.svoboda.mobi/a/levin/25200851.html.

32. Vladimir Ivakhnenko, "Vradievka: cherno-krasnaya zarya vosstaniya," Svoboda.org, June 7, 2013, http://www.svoboda.org/content/article/25038205.html.

33. "Svobodivets': Militsioneri Vradiivki za 3 roki zgvaltuvali I vbili 5 zhinok," *Ukrains'ka Pravda,* July 3, 2013.

34. David Satter, "Zoopark Yanukovych," *Kievsky dnevnik* chast' 5, Svoboda. org, December 19, 2013, http://www.svoboda.org/content/article/25206503.html.

35. "Ukrainian Activists Fear Kidnapping, Beatings, and Death," DW.De, January 27, 2014, http://www.dw.com/en/ukrainian-activists-fear-kidnapping-beatings-and-death/a-17388514; "Euromaidan Activist Reappears as Casualties Rise in Ukraine," www.freedomhouse.org, January 31, 2014, https://freedomhouse.org/article/euromaidan-activist-reappears-casualties-rise-ukraine#.VfHySxFViko.

36. "Ukrainians Bring Down Yanukovych Regime, 2013–2014," Global Nonviolent Action Database, November 2013–February 2014, http://nvdatabase. swarthmore.edu/content/ukrainians-bring-down-yanukovych-regime-2013-2014.

37. "Ukraine: Deadly Clashes Around Parliament in Kiev," BBC.co.uk, February 18, 2004, http://www.bbc.com/news/world-europe-26236860.

38. "At Least Four Reported Dead, More Than 100 Injured as Violent Clashes Break Out Near Ukraine's Parliament," *Kyiv Post,* February 18, 2014.

39. "Ukraine Crisis: Timeline," BBC News, November 13, 2014, www.bbc.co.uk/news/world-middle-east-26248275.

40. Andrei Kurkov, *Ukraine Diaries: Dispatches from Kiev,* trans. Sam Taylor (London: Harvill Secker, 2014), 118.

41. "Ukrainians Bring Down Yanukovych Regime." According to the Ukrainian Health Ministry, the death toll was twenty-eight. "MOZ: S nachala stolknovenii pogiblo 28 chelovek," *Ukrainskaya Pravda,* February 20, 2014.

42. Kurkov, *Ukraine Diaries,* 118.

43. "MOZ: S nachala stolknovenii pogiblo 28 chelovek."

44. "Ukrainians Bring Down Yanukovych Regime."

45. Kurkov, *Ukraine Diaries,* 120.

46. See Gabriel Gatehouse, "The Untold Story of the Maidan Massacre," *BBC News Magazine,* www.bbc.co.uk/news/magazine-31359021; Steve Stecklow and Oleksandr Akymenko, "Special Report: Flaws Found in Ukraine's Probe of Maidan Massacre," Reuters, October 10, 2014.

47. Ian Traynor, "Ukraine's Bloodiest Day: Dozens Dead as Kiev Protesters Regain Territory from Police," *Guardian,* February 21, 2014.

48. Ibid.

49. Vechnaya Pamyat' Pogibshim Pravookhranitelyam, Ministerstvo Vnutrennikh Del, Ukraine, March 3, 2014, http://www.mvs.gov.ua/mvs/control/main/ru/publish/article/989615.

50. Andrew Higgins and Andrew E. Kramer, "Ukraine Leader Was Defeated Even Before He Was Ousted," *New York Times,* January 3, 2015.

51. Ibid.

52. Adrian Shaw, "Vladimir Putin Boasts of Planning Ukraine Invasion as He Vowed to Bring Crimea Back to Russia," www.mirror.co.uk, March 9, 2015, http://www.mirror.co.uk/news/world-news/vladimir-putin-boasts-planning-ukraine-5301238.

53. Vladimir Voronov, "Crimea and the Kremlin: From Plan 'A' to Plan 'B,' " Henry Jackson Society, March 25, 2015, henryjacksonsociety.org/2015/03/23/crimea-and-the-kremlin-from-plan-a-to-plan-b/.

54. Ibid.

55. Valery Shiryaev, "Krym. God spustya. Chto my znaem teper,' " *Novaya Gazeta*, February 20, 2015.

56. "Crimea Declares Independence, Seeks UN Recognition," RT.com, March 17, 2014, http://www.rt.com/news/crimea-referendum-results-official-250/.

57. "Voter Turnout at Pseudo-Referendum in Crimea Was Maximum 30–40 Percent—Mejlis," Ukrinform.ua, March 17, 2014, http://www.ukrinform.ua/end/news/voter_turnout_at_pseudo_referendum_in_crimea_was_maximum_30_40 percent of voters.

58. Oleg Shynkarenko, "Putin's Crimea Propaganda Machine," Daily Beast, March 3, 2014, http://www.thedailybeast.com/articles/2014/03/03/putin-s-crimea-propaganda-machine.html.

59. Address by President of the Russian Federation, President of Russia, March 18, 2014, en.Kremlin.ru/events/president/news/20603.

60. Jack Moore, "Ukraine Crisis: Putin Approval Rating Hits 3-Year High After Crimea Invasion and Sochi Olympics," www.ibtimes.co.uk, March 13, 2014, http://www.ibtimes.co.uk/ukraine-crisis-putin-approval-rating-hits-3-year-high-after-crimea-invasion-sochi-olympics-1440113.

61. Voronov, "Crimea and the Kremlin."

62. Ibid.

63. Ibid.

64. Alexander Prokhanov, "Kto ty 'Strelok'?," interview with Yegor Strelkov, *Zavtra*, November 20, 2014.

65. David Blair, "Ukraine Crisis: Rebels Claim High Turnout and Landslide 'Yes' Vote in Plebiscite on Independence," *Telegraph*, May 11, 2014.

66. "Strelkov Declared Supreme Commander," Ukrainian Policy, May 12, 2014.www.ukrainianpolicy.com/donetsk-republic-coup-strelkov-girkin-now-supreme-commander/.

67. "Referendum Results in Donetsk and Lugansk Regions Show Landslide Support for Self-Rule," RT.com, May 11, 2014, http://www.rt.com/news/158276-referendum-results-east-ukraine/.

68. Voronov, "Crimea and the Kremlin."

69. Ibid.

70. Luke Harding, "Uneasy Standoff in Ukraine's pro-Russian Stronghold of Slvayansk," *Guardian*, April 24, 2014.

71. Lucian Kim, "Should Putin Fear the Man Who 'Pulled the Trigger of War' in Ukraine?" Reuters.com, November 26, 2014, http://www.reuters.com/article/idUSL2N0TG1CM20141126.

72. "Ves' bred rossiiskikh SMI za god," *Svobodnaya Zona,* January 11, 2015, http://www.szona.org/ves-bred-rossijskih-smi-za-god/.

73. Alexandra Vagner and Andrei Korolyev, " 'Armiya SOS' i 'Voenkomat DNR'—Radio Svoboda viyasnilo, kto I kak pomogaet voyuyushchim storonam na vostoke Ukraini," Svoboda.org, July 30, 2014, http://www.svoboda.mobi/a/25475290.html.

74. Ibid.

75. "Ya prinyal reshenie narushit raspisku o nerazglashenii . . ." Znak.com, August 25, 2014, rpt. in www.anti.kor.com.ua, August 26, 2014, http://antikor.com.ua/articles/12085-ja_prinjal_reshenie_narushitj_raspisku_o_nerazglashenii.

76. "Uraltsi uekhali voevat na Donbass. Svyashchenniki za: 'Beite fashistskuyu svoloch,' " UralPolit.ru, March 12, 2015, http://uralpolit.ru/news/sverdl/12-03-2015/57158.

77. "Kontraktniki iz Murmanska ne zakhotei ekhat v Ukrainu," February 14, 2015, http://newsland.com/news/detail/id/1499903/; Vladimir Dergachev, Denis Telmanov, and Andrei Vinokurov, "Tam russkiye gibnut, vy dozhni ikh zashchishchat," Gazeta.ru, February 13, 2015, http://www.gazeta.ru/politics/2015/02/11_a_6408545.shtml.

78. Viktor Rezunkov, "Neizvestnie soldati tainoi voini," Svoboda.org, January 23, 2015, http://www.svoboda.org/content/article/26809300.html.

79. Irena Chalupa, "Russia Secretively Buries Its Soldiers Killed in the Ukraine War," Ukraine Alert, August 28, 2014, http://www.atlanticcouncil.org/blogs/new-atlanticist/russia-secretively-buries-its-soldiers-killed-in-the-Ukraine-war.

80. Ibid.

81. Terrence McCoy, "Russian Troops Fighting in Ukraine? Naw. They're Just on 'Vacation,' " *Washington Post,* August 28, 2014.

82. Ivan Zhilin, "Voina. Obratnaya svyaz,' " *Novaya Gazeta,* March 2, 2015.

83. "Na granitze idyet voina na dva fronta: protiv terroristov i protiv rossiiskikh voisk—Tymchuk," www.inforesist.org, July 22, 2014, http://inforesist.org/na-granice-idet-vojna-na-dva-fronta-protiv-terroristov-i-protiv-rossijskix-vojsk-tymchuk/.

84. Andrew E. Kramer and Michael R. Gordon, "Russia Sent Tanks to Separatists in Ukraine, U.S. Says," *New York Times,* June 13, 2014; "Ukraine Wants Russia to Explain How MANPADS from the Russian Military Base Came to the Separatists in Donbas," lifeinua.info, June 18, 2014, http://lifeinua.info/ukraine-

demands-an-explanation-from-russia-on-how-manpads-igla-from-the-russian-military-base-turned-out-to-be-in-donbass/.

85. Margaret Coker and Robert Wall, "Ukraine Knew of Separatists' Air-Defense Capabilities, Say Officials," *Wall Street Journal,* July 19, 2014.

86. Ibid.

87. Tatyana Lokshina, "Civilians Despair as Both Sides Break the Rules in East Ukraine," *Moscow Times,* December 24, 2014.

88. Anna Nemtsova, "Why Is Ukraine's War So Bloody? The Soviet Union Trained Both Sides," Daily Beast, February 3, 2015, http://www.thedailybeast.com/articles/2015/02/03/why-is-ukraine-s-war-so-bloody-the-soviet-union-trained-both-sides.html.

## 6. Russia's Fate

1. Jim Heintz, "Putin: Russia Prepared Raising Nuclear Readiness over Crimea," Associated Press, March 15, 2015.

2. Umberto Bacchi, "Russia Issues Nuclear Threat over Crimea and Baltic States," *International Business Times,* April 2, 2015.

3. Julian Isherwood, "Russia Warns Denmark Its Warships Could Become Nuclear Targets," *Telegraph,* March 21, 2015.

4. "Polkovnik FSB: Sledite za novostyami—kto iz priblizhennikh k Putinu 'vnezapno' pogibnet v DTP, aviakatastrophe ili no okhote," Gordonua.com, March 13, 2015, http://gordonua.com/publications/Polkovnik-FSB-Sledite-za-novostyami-kto-iz-priblizhennyh-k-Putinu-vnezapno-pogibnet-v-DTP-aviakatastrofe-ili-na-ohote-70853.html.

5. Ibid.

6. Denis Volkov, "Putin's Ratings: Anomaly or Trend?" *Institute of Modern Russia,* December 23, 2014, imrussia.org/en/analysis/nation/2135-putins-ratings-anomaly-or-trend.

7. "Vladimir Putin Phone-in: Western Sanctions Actually Helped Russia," *Telegraph,* April 16, 2015.

8. Karen Dawisha, *Putin's Kleptocracy: Who Owns Russia* (New York: Simon and Schuster, 2014), 321.

9. Anders Aslund, "Russia in Free Fall," *Capital,* February 2, 2015, https://piie.com/publications/opeds/print.cfm?ResearchId=2756&doc=pub.

10. Ibid.

11. "Russia Inflation Tops 11 percent," *Moscow Times,* January 11, 2015.

12. "Russia: Vodka Minimum Price Cut over Economic Woes," BBC.co.uk, February 3, 2015, http://www.bbc.com/news/blogs-news-from-elsewhere-31109471.

13. "Vot pochemu boevikov khoronyat ne nad Donbasse, a v Rostove," uainfo. org, April 2, 2015, uainfo.org/blognews/52231-vot-pochimu-boevikov-hoornyat-ne-na-donbasse-a-v-rostove-foto.html.

14. "Boeviki DNR i LNR imeyut stol'ko zhe tankov, skol'ko armii Germanii, Frantsii i Chekhii vmeste vzyatie," www.inforesist.org, April 12, 2015, http://inforesist. org/boeviki-dnr-i-lnr-imeyut-stolko-zhe-tankov-skolko-armii-germanii-francii-i-chexii-vmeste-vzyatye/.

15. Vladislav Inozemtsev, "Kak rukhnet rezhim. Vozmozhnyi stsenarii," Slon. ru, January 5, 2015, http://slon.ru/insights/1202339/.

16. "Zhena oligarcha: vse nam prosto zaviduyut, a mwi poteshaemsya," www. spr.ru, December 24, 2014, http://www.spr.ru/novosti/2014-12/zhena-oligarha-vse-nam-prosto–zaviduyut-a-mi-poteshaemsya.html.

17. Satter, "Ukraine's Revolutionary Lesson for Russia," Daily Beast, March 2, 2014, http://www.thedailybeast.com/articles/2014/03/02/ukraine-s-revolutionary-less-for-russia.html.

# Bibliography

"Address by President of the Russian Federation." en.kremlin.ru, March 18, 2014, en.Kremlin.ru/events/president/news/20603.

Akhmadov, Ilyas, and Miriam Lanskoy. *The Chechen Struggle: Independence Won and Lost.* New York: Palgrave Macmillan, 2010.

Aslund, Anders. "Russia in Free Fall." *Capital,* February 2, 2015, https://piie.com/publicatgions/opeds/print.cfm?ResearchId=2756&doc=pub.

———. "Tri Osnovye Istochniki Bogatstva Novykh Russkikh." *Izvestiya,* June 20, 1996.

———. "Unmasking President Putin's Grandiose Myth." *Moscow Times,* November 28, 2007.

"At Least Four Reported Dead, More than 100 Injured as Violent Clashes Break Out Near Ukraine's Parliament." *Kyiv Post,* February 18, 2014.

Bacchi, Umberto. "Russia Issues Nuclear Threat over Crimea and Baltic States." *International Business Times,* April 2, 2015.

Baker, Peter, and Susan Glasser. *Kremlin Rising.* New York: Scribner, 2005.

Bashkirova, Valeriya, Alexander Solovyev, and Vladislav Dorofeev. *Geroi 90-x: Lyudi i Den'gi, Noveishaya Istoriya Kapitalisma v Rossii.* Moscow: Kommersant and ANF, 2012.

Batumsky, Andrei. "Sgovor." *Versiya,* August 3, 1999.

Baturin, Y. M., et al. *Epokha El'tsina: ocherki politicheskoi istorii.* Moscow: Vagrius, 2001.

Bennetts, Marc. "Faith Healer Anatoly Kashpirovsky: Russia's New Rasputin." *Observer,* June 6, 2010.

Bivens, Matt. "Ballot Fraud: Not If, but How Much." *Moscow Times,* June 4, 1996.

"Biznesmen Andrei Lugovoy—o 'delo Litvinenko': 'Pochemu Ya dolzhen vsye brosat I nestis' v Angliyu?' " *Izvestiya,* February 26, 2007, http://izvestia.ru/news/322036.

Blair, David. "Ukraine Crisis: Rebels Claim High Turnout and Landslide 'Yes' Vote in Plebiscite on Independence." *Telegraph,* May 11, 2014.

"Boeviki DNR i LNR imeyut stol'ko zhe tankov, skol'ko armii Germanii, Frantsii I Chekhii vmeste vzyatie." www.inforesist.org, April 12, 2015, http://inforesist.org/boeviki-dnr-i-lnr-imeyut-stolko-zhe-tankov-skolko-armii-germanii-francii-i-chexii-vmeste-vzyatye/.

Bogoran, Irina, and Andrei Soldatov. "Nepravda." *Versiya,* November 4–10, 2002.

Bowring, Bill. "Judicial Independence in Russia." *EU-Russia Review,* no. 1, May 2006.

Browder, Bill. *Red Notice: How I Became Putin's No. 1 Enemy,* London: Bantam Press, 2015.

Bullough, Oliver. "Putin Vows No Deal with 'Terrorists' After Siege." Reuters, October 28, 2002.

Chalupa, Irena. "Russia Secretively Buries Its Soldiers Killed in the Ukraine War." Atlantic Council, August 28, 2014, http://www.atlanticcouncil.org/blogs/new-atlanticist/russia-secretively-buries-its-soldiers-killed-in-ukraine-war.

Chazan, Guy. "In Russia's Courts, a Judge Speaks Up and Gets Fired." *Wall Street Journal,* August 5, 2004.

"Chto eto bylo? Spasenie Zalozhnikov ili Unichtozhenie Terroristov." *Novaya Gazeta,* no. 86, November 21, 2002.

Clarke, Renfrey. "Russian Miners Demand: 'Yeltsin Out.' " *Green Left Weekly,* June 19, 1998.

Clover, Charles. "A Death Retold." *Financial Times,* February 19, 2009.

———. "Russia's Middle Class Finds Its Feet." *Financial Times,* December 12, 2011.

Cockburn, Patrick. "Russia Planned Chechen War Before Bombings." *Independent,* January 29, 2000.

Coker, Margaret, and Robert Wall. "Ukraine Knew of Separatists' Air-Defense Capabilities, Say Officials." *Wall Street Journal,* July 19, 2014.

Colton, Timothy J., and Michael McFaul. *Popular Choice and Managed Democracy: The Russian Elections of 1999 and 2000.* Washington, D.C.: Brookings Institution Press, 2003.

"Crimea Declares Independence, Seeks UN Recognition." RT.com, March 17, 2014, https://pressall.wordpress.com/2014/03/page/12/.

Curtis, Glenn Eldon. *Russia: A Country Study.* Washington, D.C.: Library of Congress, Federal Research Division, 1998.

Dawisha, Karen. *Putin's Kleptocracy: Who Owns Russia?* New York: Simon and Schuster, 2014.

"Delo Anni Politkovskoi: Zakazchik poka 'neprikasaemii.'" *Novaya Gazeta,* December 12, 2012.

Dergachev, Vladimir, Denis Telmanov, and Andrei Vinokurov. "Tam russkiye gibnut, vy dozhni ikh zashchishchat." Gazeta.ru, February 13, 2015, http://www.gazeta.ru/politics/2015/02/11_a_6408545.shtml.

Doklad deputatskoi komissii Parlamenta RSO-Alaniya po rassmotrenniyu I vyyaneniyu obstoyatel'stv, svyannikh s tragicheskimi sobitiyami v g. Beslan 1–3 Centyabrya 2004 goda, 18–19, available at http://www.pravdabeslana.ru/trigoda/doklad.htm.

Donskikh, Ilya, "Moskva. Sostoyalas' press-konferentsiya, nosvyashchennaya zavershivshemusya sudebnomu razbiratel'stvu po delu ob ubiistve Anni Politkovskoi i opravdatel'nomu verdiktu prisazhnikh, vynesennomu segodnya, *Novaya Gazeta,* No. 17 ot February 18, 2009.

Dunlop, JohnB. *The Moscow Bombings of September 1999.* Stuttgart: ibidem-Verlag, 2012.

Dunlop, John B., *The 2002 Dubrovka and 2004 Beslan Hostage Crises: A Critique of Russian Counter-Terrorism.* Stuttgart: ibidem-Verlag, 2006.

"Euromaidan Activist Reappears as Casualties Rise in Ukraine." www.freedomhouse.org, January 31, 2014, https://freedomhouse.org/article/euromaidan-activist-reappears-casualties-rise-ukraine.

Felgenhauer, Pavel. "Putinskaya operatsiya spaseniyu zalozhnikov vyzivaet mnogo voprosov." Inopressa.ru, trans. and rpt. from *Wall Street Journal,* November 1, 2002.

Felshtinsky, Yuri, and Vladimir Pribylovsky. *The Corporation: Russia and the KGB in the Age of President Putin.* New York and London: Encounter, 2008.

Fenton, Ben, John Steele, Roger Highfield, and Duncan Gardham. "Net Tightens on the Amateur Assassins." *Telegraph,* December 1, 2006.

Feshbach, Murray. "Russia's Population Meltdown," *Wilson Quarterly,* Winter 2001, http://archive.wilsonquarterly.com/sites/default/files/articles/WQ_VOL25_W_2001_Article_01.pdf.

Gall, Carlotta, and Thomas de Waal, *Chechnya: Calamity in the Caucasus.* New York: New York University Press, 1998.

Gatehouse, Gabriel. "The Untold Story of the Maidan Massacre." *BBC News Magazine,* February 12, 2015, www.bbc.co.uk/news/magazine-31359021.

Gessen, Masha. *The Man Without a Face.* New York: Riverhead, 2012.

Glinkina, Svetlana. "The Criminal Components of the Russian Economy," Working paper no. 29, *Berichte des Bundesinstituts fur Ostwissenschaftliche und Internationale Studien,* 1997.

Glinkina, Svetlana, Andrei Grigoriev, and Vakhtang Yakobidze. "Crime and Corruption," in *The New Russia: Transition Gone Awry,* ed. Lawrence R. Klein and Marshall Pomer, 233–50. Stanford, Calif.: Stanford University Press, 2000.

Goldfarb, Alex, with Marina Litvinenko. *Death of a Dissident.* New York: Free Press, 2007.

Gorbacheva, Ada. "Poka Nadeyus—Dyshu." *Nezavisimaya Gazeta,* January 26, 2001.

Grafova, Lidiya. "Chtoby nigde i nikogda." *Novaya Gazeta,* August 29, 2005.
———. "Nado zhe Komu-to Verit." *Novaya Gazeta,* September 15, 2005.

Gubareva, Svetlana. "Vystuplenie na press konferentsii k tretei godovshchine, 'Nord Ost' Tragediya na Dubrovke." Zalozhniki.ru, October 25, 2005, www.zalozhniki.ru/comment/9718.html.

Gubareva, Svetlana, Karina Moskalenko, and Olga Mikhailova. " 'Nord-Ost,' Gaz ne spasal ot vzriva." *Novaya Gazeta,* March 21, 2005.

Gupta, R. C, *Collapse of the Soviet Union.* Meerut: Krishna Prakashan Media, 1997.

Grafova, Lidiya. "Chtoby nigde i nikogda." *Novaya Gazeta,* August 29, 2005.

Grigoriants, Sergei. "Napravo krugom marsh . . ." grigoryants.ru, October 4, 2013, http://grigoryants.ru/sovremennaya-diskussiya/chuma-na-oba-vashix-doma.

Gudkov, Lev. "Who Is to Blame for Things Going Badly for Us?" *Novaya Gazeta,* September 21, 2011.

Harding, Luke. "Anna Politkovskaya Trial: The Unanswered Questions." *Guardian,* February 19, 2009.

———. "Putin, the Kremlin Power Struggle, and the $40 bn Fortune." *Guardian,* December 21, 2007.

———. "Uneasy Standoff in Ukraine's Pro-Russian Stronghold of Slavyansk." *Guardian,* April 24, 2014.

Heintz, Jim. "Putin: Russia Prepared Raising Nuclear Readiness over Crimea." Associated Press, March 15, 2015.

Higgins, Andrew, and Andrew E. Kramer. "Ukraine Leader Was Defeated Even Before He Was Ousted." *New York Times,* January 3, 2015.

Hill, Fiona, and Clifford G. Gaddy. *Mr. Putin: Operative in the Kremlin.* Washington, D.C.: Brookings Institution Press, 2013.

Hoffman, David E. *The Oligarchs: Wealth and Power in the New Russia.* New York: Public Affairs, 2011.

Illarionov, Andrei. Testimony before the U.S. House of Representatives Committee on Foreign Affairs, February 25, 2009.

Inozemtsev, Vldislav. "Kak rukhnet rezhim. Vozmozhnyi stsenarii." Slon. ru, January 5, 2015. http://slon.ru/insights/1202339/

Ioffe, Julia. "Net Impact: One Man's Cyber-Crusade Against Russian Corruption." *New Yorker,* April 4, 2011.

Isherwood, Julian. "Russia Warns Denmark Its Warships Could Become Nuclear Targets." *Telegraph,* March 21, 2015.

Ivakhnenko, Vladimir. "Vradievka: cherno-krasnaya zarya vosstaniya." Svoboda.org, June 7, 2013.

Jeffries, Ian. *The New Russia: A Handbook of Economic and Political Developments.* New York: Routledge, 2002.

Judah, Ben. *Fragile Empire: How Russia Fell in and out of Love with Vladimir Putin.* New Haven: Yale University Press, 2013.

Kanev, Sergei. "Kak ustroeni 'kryshi' v Rossii." *Novaya Gazeta,* October 22, 2007.

Kara-Murza, Vladimir. "Russia's Rigged Election." *Wall Street Journal Europe,* June 28, 2011.

Kara-Murza, Vladimir. "Stealing the Vote: The Kremlin Fixes Another Election," *World Affairs,* September–October 2011.

Kazanskyi, Denys. "Akhmetov's Losing Bet." *Ukrainian Week,* May 18, 2015.

Kendall, Bridget. "Russia's Putin Shines at Valdai Summit as He Castigates West." www.bbc.co.uk, September 20, 2013, http://www.bbc.co.uk/news/world-europe-24170137.

Khinshtein, Alexandr. "Chernye vdovy pod 'kryshei' Petrovki." *Moskovsky Komsomolets,* July 23, 2003.

Kim, Lucian. "Should Putin Fear the Man who 'Pulled the Trigger of War' in Ukraine?" Reuters.com, November 26, 2014, http://www.reuters.com/article/idUSL2N0TG1CM20141126.

Kislinskaya, Larisa. "Kto otvetit za bazaar?" *Sovershenno Sekretno,* April 1, 2006.

Knight, Amy. "Who Killed Politkovskaya?" *New York Review of Books,* no. 17, November 6, 2008.

"Kontrakti iz Murmansk ne zakhoteli ekhat v Ukrainu." Newsland.ru, February 14, 2015, http://newsland.com/news/detail/id/1499903/.

Korol'kov, Igor. "Fotorobot ne pervoi svezhosti." *Moskovskie novosti,* November 11, 2003.

———. "U nego ne bylo shansov vyzhit." Svoboda.org, July 20, 2014, http://www.svoboda.org/content/article/25462059.html#page=1.

Kramer, A. "The Role of the Masses During the October 1993 Moscow Rebellion." www. Marxist.com, October 6, 2003, http://www.marxist.com/1993-moscow-rebellion-masses.htm.

Kramer, Andrew E., and Michael R. Gordon. "Russia Sent Tanks to Separatists in Ukraine, U.S. Says." *New York Times,* June 13, 2014.

Kurkov, Andrei. *Ukraine Diaries: Dispatches from Kiev.* Trans. Sam Taylor. London: Harvill Secker, 2014.

Levchenko, Alexei, and Lev Moskovsky. "Seleznev znaet, kto zryval Rossiyu." *Noviye izvestiya,* March 21, 2002.

LeVine, Steve. *Putin's Labyrinth: Spies, Murder, and the Dark Heart of the New Russia.* New York: Random House Trade Paperbacks, 2009.

Litvinenko, Alexander, and Yuri Felshtinsky. *Blowing Up Russia: Terror from Within.* New York: S.P.I. Books, 2002.

Lokshina, Tatyana. "Civilians Despair as Both Sides Break the Rules in East Ukraine," *Moscow Times,* December 24, 2014.

Malkov, Igor. "Prodavets 'Razrezhennyi Vozdukh': Den'gi Mozhet Byt ne Tol'ko 'Derevyannyie no Tozhe Berezovskyi' " *Moskovsky Komsomolets,* July 31, 1997.

"MANPADS from Russian Military Base Are Used by Terrorists in Donbas: Foreign Ministry Demands Explanation from Russia." Censor.net, June 18, 2014, http://en.censor.net.ua/photo_news/290463/manpads_ from_russian_military_base_are_used_by_terrorists_in_donbas_foreign_ ministry_demands_explanation.

McCoy, Terrence. "Russian Troops Fighting in Ukraine? Naw. They're Just on 'Vacation.' " *Washington Post,* August 28, 2014.

McFaul, M., and N. Petrov, eds. *The Political Almanac of Russia, 1997.* Vol. 1, *Elections and Political Development.* Moscow: Carnegie Endowment for International Peace, 1998.

Medvedev, Roy. *Kapitalism v Rossii?* Moscow: Prava Cheloveka, 1998.

———. *Vladimir Putin: chetire goda v Kremle.* Moscow: Vremya, 2004.

———. *Vremya Putina?* Moscow: Prava Cheloveka, 2001.

Milashina, Elena. "Agentura vyshla uz-pod kontrolya. I Dosha do Beslana." *Novaya Gazeta,* August 31, 2009.

"Minister yustitsii Alexander Konovalov: uvazehnie k zakonu v povsednevnoi zhizni v Rossii ne bylo nikogda." polit.ru, June 2, 2008, http://polit.ru/ article/2008/06/02/interview/.

Moore, Jack. "Ukraine Crisis: Putin Approval Rating Hits 3-Year High After Crimea Invasion and Sochi Olympics." *International Business Times,* March 13, 2014, http://www.ibtimes.co.uk/ukraine-crisis-putin-approval-rating-hits-3-year-high-after-crimea-invasion-sochi-olympics-1440113.

Mursalieva, Galina. "Ubival ne tol'ko gaz—Ubivalo Vremya," interview with Alexander Shabalov, director, Moskovsky Sluzhbi Spasenie. *Novaya Gazeta,* November 4–10, 2002.

"MOZ: S nachala stolknovenii pogiblo 28 chelovek." *Ukrainskaya Pravda,* February 20, 2014.

"Na granitze idyet voina na dva fronta: protiv terroristov i protiv rossiiskikh voisk—Tymchuk." *www.inforesist.org,* July 22, 2014, http://inforesist. org/na-granice-idet-vojna-na-dva-fronta-protiv-terroristov-i-protiv-rossijskix-vojsk-tymchuk/.

"Natalya Estemirova Kidnapped in Grozny, Found Dead in Ingushetiya," *Eurasia Daily Monitor,* May 16, 2009.

Nedkov, Vesselin, and Paul Wilson. *57 Hours: A Survivor's Account of the Moscow Hostage Drama.* Toronto: Viking Canada, 2003.

Nemtsov, Boris, and Leonid Martynyuk. "Winter Olympics in the Sub-Tropics: Corruption and Abuse in Sochi." Trans. Catherine A. Fitzpatrick. *Interpreter,* December 6, 2013.

Nemtsov, Boris, and Vladimir Milov. "Putin: The Bottom Line." Trans. David Essel, rpt. in www.larussophobe.com, March 31, 2008, https:// larussophobe.wordpress.com/2008/03/31/boris-nemtsovs-white-paper-in-full/.

———. *Putin: What Ten Years of Putin Have Brought: An Independent Expert Report.* Trans. David Essel. Moscow: Solidarnost, 2010.

Nemtsova, Anna. "Why Is Ukraine's War So Bloody? The Soviet Union Trained Both Sides." Daily Beast, February 3, 2015, http://www. thedailybeast.com/articles/2015/02/03/why-is-ukraine-s-war-so-bloody-the-soviet-union-trained-both-sides.html.

"Operatinnaya soprovozhdenie ubiistva." *Novaya Gazeta,* no. 74, October 6, 2008.

Osborn, Andrew. "All-Female Sect Worships Vladimir Putin as Paul the Apostle." *Telegraph,* May 12, 2011.

Palmer, Richard L. Testimony before the U.S. House of Representatives Banking and Financial Services Committee, September 21, 1999.

Pan, Philip P. "3 Acquitted in Killing of Russian Reporter." *Washington Post,* February 20, 2009.

Pavlov, Dmitri. "Zayavil nachal'nik UFSB v godovshchinu vzryva na Gur'yanove." *Kommersant,* September 8, 2000.

Phillips, Timothy. *Beslan: The Tragedy of School No. 1.* London: Granta Books, 2007.

Piontkovsky, Andrei. "Rassledovanie: Priznanie Oligarkha Prokuroru Respubliki." *Novaya Gazeta,* January 21, 2001.

Podrabinek, Alexander. "Politika na Krovi." *Prima News,* November 5, 2002.

"Polkovnik FSB: Sledite za novostyami—kto iz priblizhennikh k Putinu 'vnezapno' pogibnet v DTP, aviakatastrophe ili no okhote." Gordonua. com, March 13, 2015, http://gordonua.com/publications/Polkovnik-FSB-Sledite-za-novostyami-kto-iz-priblizhennyh-k-Putinu-vnezapno-pogibnet-v-DTP-aviakatastrofe-ili-na-ohote-70853.html.

Preliminary Report, Association GOLOS—Domestic Monitoring of Elections of the President of the Russian Federation. www.golos.org, March 4, 2012, https://www.ndi.org/files/Golos-Prelim-Report-030512-ENG.pdf.

"Privatization, Russian-Style." *Nezavisimaya Gazeta—Politekonomiya, Johnson's Russia List,* April 17, 2001.

Prokhanov, Alexander. "Kto ty 'Strelok'?" interview with Igor Strelkov. *Zavtra,* November 20, 2014.

Proshkin, Leonid. "Shturm kotorogo ne bylo." *Sovershenno Sekretno,* no. 9, 1998.

"Putin: Russia Must Be Strong to Withstand Foreign Threats." Radio Free Europe/Radio Liberty, April 21, 2011.

"Putin ne doekhal do razrushennoi shkoly." *Gazeta.ru,* September 5, 2004, http://www.kavkaz-uzel.ru/articles/61146/.

Rassledovanie. "Poslednyaya Zhertva Solonika." *Express Gazeta,* no. 20, 1997.

Reddaway, Peter, and Dmitri Glinski. *The Tragedy of Russia's Reforms: Market Bolshevism Against Democracy.* Washington, D.C.: United States Institute of Peace Press, 2001.

"Referendum Results in Donetsk and Lugansk Regions Show Landslide Support for Self-Rule." RT.com, May 11, 2014, http://www.rt.com/news/158276-referendum-results-east-ukraine/.

Reznik, Genri. "Kodaneva ogovorili." Grani.ru, March 17, 2004, http://grani.ru/Politics/Russia/m.63911.html.

Rezunkov, Viktor. "Neizvestnie soldati tainoi voini." Svoboda.org, January 23, 2015, http://www.svoboda.org/content/article/26809300.html.

Rozhnov, Georgy. "Osobye Primety: Krasivaya i Molodaya." *Kriminalnaya Khronika,* March 1998.

"Russia: Vodka Minimum Price Cut over Economic Woes." *BBC.co.uk,* February 3, 2015, http://www.bbc.com/news/blogs-news-from-else-where-31109471.

"Russia Inflation Tops 11 per cent." *Moscow Times,* January 11, 2015.

*Russia, Press Country Profile.* European Court of Human Rights, July 2014, www.echr.coe.int/Documents/CP_Russia_ENG.pdf.

"Russia's Raiders." *BusinessWeek,* June 5, 2008.

Satter, David. *Age of Delirium: The Decline and Fall of the Soviet Union.* New Haven: Yale University Press, 2001.

———. "Anatomy of a Massacre." *Washington Times,* October 29, 1999.

———. *Darkness at Dawn: The Rise of the Russian Criminal State.* New Haven: Yale University Press, 2003.

———. "Death in Moscow." National Review Online, October 29, 2002.

———. "Journalism of Intimidation." Forbes, com, July 7, 2009, http://www.forbes.com/2009/07/07/paul-klebnikov-murder-opinions-david-satter.html.

———. "Krizis i Sem'ya Yanukovycha." Kievsky dnevnik, chast' 4, Svoboda.org, December 14, 2013, http://www.svoboda.mobi/a/levin/25200851.html.

——. "Kuda ukhodit ukrainskii oligarkh." Kievsky dnevnik, chast' 3, Svoboda.org, December 10, 2013, http://www.svoboda.mobi/a/us-terror-threat/25196402.html.

——. "A Low, Dishonest Decadence." National Interest, Summer 2003.

——. "Putin in Charge." *Wall Street Journal Europe,* December 13, 2007.

——. "Remembering Beslan." Forbes.com, October 1, 2009, www.forbes.com/2009/10/01/beslan-putin-politkovskaya-basaev-dzasokhov-chechen-opinions-contributors-david-satter.html.

——. "Russia's Choice." *National Review,* July 30, 2012.

——. *Russia's Looming Crisis.* Philadelphia: Foreign Policy Research Institute, March, 2012.

——. Testimony Before the U.S. House of Representatives Foreign Affairs Committee, May 24, 2007, http://www.hoover.org/sites/default/files/uploads/inline/docs/sat051707.pdf.

——. "The Truth About Beslan." *Weekly Standard,* November 13, 2006.

——. "Ukraine's Revolutionary Lesson for Russia." Daily Beast, March 2, 2014, http://www.thedailybeast.com/articles/2014/03/02/ukraine-s-revolutionary-less-for-russia.html.

——. "Who Killed Litvinenko." *Wall Street Journal,* November 27, 2006.

——. "Who Murdered These Russian Journalists?" Forbes.com, December 26, 2008, http://www.forbes.com/2008/12/24/russian-journalists-killed-oped-cx_ds_1226satter.html.

——. "Yeltsin: Shadow of a Doubt." *National Interest,* Winter 1993–94.

——. "Zoopark Yanukovych," Kievsky dnevnik, chast' 5, Svoboda.org, December 19, 2013, http://www.svoboda.org/content/article/25206503.html.

"Shamil Basaev: 'U nas est mnogo, chto rasskazat' po Beslanu . . .' " Kavkazcenter.net, August 31, 2005, http://www.kavkazcenter.com/russ/content/2005/08/31/37225/shamil-basaev-u-nas-est-mnogo-chto-rasskazat-po-beslanu——.shtml.

Shaw, Adrian. "Vladimir Putin Boasts of Planning Ukraine Invasion as He Vowed to Bring Crimea Back to Russia." www.mirror.co.uk, March 9,

2015, http://www.mirror.co.uk/news/world-news/vladimir-putin-boasts-planning-ukraine-5301238.

Shchekochikin, Yuri. "Nezamechennye novosti nedeli kotorye menya udivili." *Novaya Gazeta,* no. 4, January 20, 2003.

Shenfield, Stephen. "On the Threshold of Disaster: The Socio-Economic Situation in Russia." *Johnson's Russia List,* July 2, 1998.

Shevtsova, Lilia. "The End of Putin's Era: Domestic Drivers of Foreign Policy." In *U.S.- Russian Relations: Is Conflict Inevitable?* a publication of Hudson Institute study group, June 26, 2007.

———. *Lonely Power: Why Russia Has Failed to Become the West and the West Is Weary of Russia.* Washington, D.C.: Carnegie Endowment for International Peace, 2010.

———. "Putinism Under Siege: Implosion, Atrophy, or Revolution." *Journal of Democracy,* July 2012.

Shiryaev, Valery. "Krym. God spustya. Chto my znaem teper'." *Novaya Gazeta,* February 20, 2015.

Shpilkin, Sergei. "Statistikii Isledovala Vybory." Gazeta.ru, December 10, 2011, http://www.gazeta.ru/science/2011/12/10_a_3922390.shtml.

Shuster, Simon. "Rewriting Russian History: Did Boris Yeltsin Steal the 1996 Presidential Election?" *Time,* February 24, 2012.

Shynkarenko, Oleg. "Putin's Crimea Propaganda Machine." Daily Beast, March 3, 2014, http://www.thedailybeast.com/articles/2014/03/03/putin-s-crimea-propaganda-machine.html.

"Silence After the Explosions." *Moskovsky Komsomolets,* January 19, 2000.

Smith, Geoffrey T. "Medvedev Puts Russia in a Choice Situation." *Wall Street Journal,* June 23, 2011.

"Spasti biznes ot repressiy: Kazhdyy biznesmen—vor?" *Moscow News,* January 17, 2012.

Spravka. "Zakhvat shkoli v Beslane. Khronika sobitii." Grani.ru, September 4, 2004, http://www.grani.ru/Events/Terrror/m.76331.html.

Stecklow, Steve, and Oleksandr Akymenko. "Special Report: Flaws Found in Ukraine's Probe of Maidan Massacre." Reuters, October 10, 2014.

"Strelkov Declared Supreme Commander," Ukrainian Policy, May 12, 2014, www.ukrainianpolicy.com/donetsk-republic-coup-strelkov-girkin-now-supreme-commander/.

"Svobodivets': Militsioneri Vradiivki za 3 roki zgvaltuvali i vbili 5 zhinok." *Ukrains'ka Pravda,* July 3, 2013.

Tarasov, Aleksandr. "Provokatsiya: Versiya sobitii 3–4 Oktyabrya 1993 v Moskve." *Skepsis,* October 2–November 13, 1993. http://scepsis.net/library/id_2571.html.

Tetrault-Farber, Gabrielle. "No Closure for Victims of Theater Hostage Crisis, 12 Years On." *Moscow Times,* October 22, 2014.

Traynor, Ian. "Ukraine's Bloodiest Day: Dozens Dead as Kiev Protesters Regain Territory from Police." *Guardian,* February 21, 2014.

Treisman, Daniel S. *After the Deluge: Regional Crises and Political Consolidation in Russia.* Ann Arbor: University of Michigan Press, 1999.

Tret'yakov, Vitaly. "Goniteli sem'i i annibaly 'Otechestva.'" *Nezavisimaya gazeta,* October 12, 1999.

"Ukraine: Deadly Clashes Around Parliament in Kiev." *BBC.co.uk,* February 18, 2004, http://www.bbc.com/news/world-europe-26236860.

"Ukrainian Activists Fear Kidnapping, Beatings, and Death." DW.De, January 27, 2014, http://www.dw.com/en/ukrainian-activists-fear-kidnapping-beatings-and-death/a-17388514.

"Ukrainians Bring Down Yanukovych Regime, 2013–2014." Global Nonviolent Action Database, November 2013–February 2014, http://nvdatabase.swarthmore.edu.

"Uraltsi uekhali voevat na Donbass. Svyashchenniki za: Beite fashistskuyu svoloch." UralPolit.ru, March 12, 2015, http://uralpolit.ru/news/sverdl/12-03-2015/57158.

Vagner, Alexandra, and Andrei Korolyev. "'Armiya SOS' i 'Voenkomat DNR'—Radio Svoboda viyasnilo, kto i kak pomogaet voyuyushchim storonam na vostoke Ukraini." Svoboda.org, July 30, 2014, http://www.svoboda.mobi/a/25475290.html.

"Vechnaya Pamyat' Pogibshim Pravookhranitelyam . . ." Ministerstvo Vnutrennykh Del Ukraina, http://www.mvs.gov.ua/mvs/control/main/ru/publish/article/989615.

"Ves' bred rossiiskikh SMI za god." *Svobodnaya Zona,* January 11, 2015, http://www.szona.org/ves-bred-rossijskih-smi-za-god/.

Vinogradov, Dmitri. "Kak Zyuganov sdal svoikh izbiratelei i pobedu v 1996," interview with Viktor Ilyukhin, *Gazeta.ru,* November 11, 2011.

"Vladimir Putin Phone-in: Western Sanctions Actually Helped Russia." *Telegraph,* April 16, 2015.

Volkov, Denis. "Putin's Ratings: Anomaly or Trend?" Institute of Modern Russia, December 23, 2014, imrussia.org/en/analysis/nation/2135-putins-ratings-anomaly-or-trend.

Voronov, Vladimir. "Crimea and the Kremlin: From Plan 'A' to Plan 'B.' " Henry Jackson Society, March 25, 2015, henryjacksonsociety.org/2015/03/23/crimea-and-the-kremlin-from-plan-a-to-plan-b/.

———. "No One Bargains with Terrorists, Do They? Beslan 10 Years Later." Trans. Irina Sadokha and David Satter. Russian Studies Centre, Henry Jackson Society, in cooperation with the Russian Service, Radio Liberty, October 2014.

"Voter Turnout at Pseudo-Referendum in Crimea Was Maximum 30–40 Percent—Mejlis." Ukrinform.ua, March 17, 2014, http://www.ukrinform.ua/end/news/voter_turnout_at_pseudo_referendum_in_crimea_was_maximum_30_40 percent_of_voters.

"Vot pochemu boevikov khoronyat ne nad Donbasse, a v Rostove." *uainfo.org,* April 2, 2015, uainfo.org/blognews/52231-vot-pochimu-boevikov-hoornyat-ne-na-donbasse-a-v-rostove-foto.html.

"V Tserkvi blagoslovit reshenie o 'mirnoi i druzheskoi' peredache vlasti ot Medvedev k Putinu." *Interfax,* September 26, 2011.

Weir, Fred. "Gas Clouds Moscow Rescue." *Christian Science Monitor,* October 28, 2002.

"Why Were Doctors in the Dark?" Editorial, *Moscow Times,* October 28, 2002.

Womack, Helen. "Return of the KGB." *Newsweek,* November 24, 2003.

Yablokova, Oksana, Simon Saradzhyan, and Lena Kor. "Apartment Block Explodes, Dozens Dead." *Moscow Times,* September 10, 1999.

"Ya prinyal reshenie narushit raspisku o nerazglashenii ..." Znak.com, August 25, 2014, rpt. at www.anti.kor.com.ua, August 26, 2014.

Zakharovich, Yuri. "Profits of Doom." *Time Europe,* October 6, 2003.

"Zhena oligarcha: vse nam prosto zaviduyut, a mwi poteshaemsya," www.spr.ru, December 24, 2014, http://www.spr.ru/novosti/2014-12/zhena-oligarha-vse-nam-prosto–zaviduyut-a-mi-poteshaemsya.html.

Zhilin, Ivan. "Voina. Obratnaya svyaz'." *Novaya Gazeta,* March 2, 2015.

# Index